MONIKA WEGLER

A Kitten's Life

A Kitten's Life

How Kittens Develop and Learn
During Their First Six Months
With Experiences and Adventures
From the Lives of Five Kittens

TEXT AND PHOTOS: MONIKA WEGLER

Contents

This Is My Territory 63

Fit for Fun 47

The Kittens Become Independent

Heading Out into the New World 81

New Friendships for Life 97

Our Little Stars:

Our five superstars were chosen from two litters totaling eleven kittens. See how these mini-tigers grow up and the big and small adventures they go through in the process.

La Bomba

A sweet fuzz ball, lively and adventurous ... on pages 4, 5, 14, 16, 42, 43, 45, 48, 55, 62, 66, 67, 69, 71, 74, 76, 80, 92, 93, 94, 108, 109

Sirena

The spitting image of Mama Isabella, and just as gentle and affectionate ... on pages 6, 14, 22, 23, 26, 36, 44, 52, 62, 67, 71, 75, 90, 100, 101

Flori

Loves peace and quiet and tasty food ... on pages 6, 10, 12, 23, 35, 40, 41, 50, 51, 53, 58, 60, 61, 64, 66, 73, 76, 80, 84, 85, 89, 90, 96, 105, 111

Sylvester

A charming, cuddly teddy bear with slightly macho affectations ... on pages 2, 5, 7, 20, 21, 24, 30, 32, 33, 37, 56, 70, 95, 102, 103

Frederick

A sensitive male with beautiful eyes ... on pages 2, 5, 18, 28, 29, 30, 57, 78, 98, 106, 107, 111

Foreword

What do a famous, successful speed skater and a famous author and photographer have in common?
A love of cats and a desire to do something to benefit the little tigers.

ANNI FRIESINGER

Animal welfare is dear to Anni Friesinger's heart. That's why she and Kai Pflaume were named the first official animal ambassadors by the German Animal Welfare League.

I have been fascinated by cats ever since I was little. I really love their independence and, of course, their elegant movements. They make us happy by being with us. Even if cats don't always do what we want them to, they still sense when we are down. They instinctively seek us out to comfort and cheer us up.

There were always cats in the house where I grew up, usually two, and often only females. We either got them straight from the animal shelter or they were given to us, or we got them for free from a neighboring farm. When I moved away from home, and after careful consideration, I decided to get my own cat, Snoopy. He was amazingly devoted and alert, and his playfulness was more like a dog's than a cat's. Unfortunately, after only three years he was run over by a car and killed. For a long time I didn't want to replace him, because for me there was no cat like him.

But I want to get involved in animal rights. My public life and my position as animal ambassador provide me with special opportunities to do that. I love cats, so it was natural for me to support *A Kitten's Life*. I wish the book success.

MONIKA WEGLER

Since 1983 Monika Wegler has lived and worked as a freelance photographer and author in Munich, Germany. Her dedication to animal welfare, especially for cats, is commendable.

I have spent my entire life with animals, learned much from them, and experienced joy through them. I see them as fellow creatures that deserve our respect and love.

My particular love is for cats, so I got the idea to write a book about the development of cute kittens. To instill this book with the quality I had in mind, I had to keep the kittens in my home, photographing them in my home studio. By the time I had all the photos ready and had written the last paragraph, nearly a year had gone by. I place high demands on my work and myself. The most important thing for my photos is to capture the nature of the animal and emphasize its personality.

The kittens and my adult cats were terrific models during the photo shoots, and they really enjoyed their work in front of the camera.

Now let me tell you the tales of La Bomba, Flori, Sirena, Sylvester, Frederick, and the other cats. All of them are special in their own way. You will also learn a lot of important information about owning and taking care of these lovable little tigers.

Monika Wegler

Mommy Is the Best

Newborn kittens are helpless and depend entirely on their mother's care. Deaf, eyes closed, they lie in their basket while their mother warms, cleans, and tirelessly suckles them, especially during the first three weeks of life. This is a full-time job that scarcely leaves the mother cat time for her own needs.

Here We Are!

IN FEBRUARY my female cat Isabella came into the love-stricken state referred to as *heat*. She rolled voluptuously on the floor, pressed her hips against us when we petted her, and called longingly for a male cat. The usually quiet, reserved cat meowed so loudly that she kept us all awake. I wanted one-year-old Isabella to have a litter, but hoped to wait a few more months before breeding her with a male. But Isabella was in a rush. And so she lured my only unneutered male cat, Dolittle, up to the loft while I continued writing, clueless, in my workroom downstairs. Because Dolittle was barely seven months old, I thought the late bloomer was too sexually immature to be dangerous. Previously he had never shown the slightest interest in female cats in heat in our presence. The rascal! After five weeks, Isabella's belly was getting larger, and the veterinarian confirmed what we could no longer overlook. With my twenty years of experience with cats, all my friends smiled mockingly. "Never trust a tomcat!" How true!

Two Expectant Mothers

I had planned to document the birth and growth of the kittens in written notes and photographs. That's where the idea for this book came from. In the meantime, my four-year-old Maine Coon cat

Flori the male cat has made it. Now the 3 ounces (80 g) of kitten gets licked with the mother's tongue to stimulate its circulatory system.

Weeks 1 through 3

Serafina had also come into heat, so I brought her to her cat lover away from the house. With her multicolored litter, she later provided color with my little velvet-pawed photo models.

The gestation period for a female cat generally lasts between sixty-two and sixty-five days, so it is possible to predict the approximate date of birth. The emphasis here is on *approximate*. First, we almost never know the exact day of conception, and second, some cats don't stick to the norm. The time of birth hangs in the balance until the last moment, and it can even hold off for up to seventy days.

Serafina and Isabella are both especially affectionate now and are spoiled with soft, circular tummy rubs. For the first few weeks we don't see much evidence of the kittens in their tummies. The nipples feel firmer and take on a dark pink color. Starting with the fifth week, I offer the mother cats four smaller meals a day rather than the usual two. With their crowded stomachs during pregnancy, they can't eat as much at one sitting. It's understandable why we spoil them even more than usual. In addition to high-quality commercial food, several times a week the two cats also get cooked chicken, fish, lamb, cream cheese with egg yolk, and about two to three tablespoons of their favorite yogurt. Both have a sweet tooth and prefer my favorite, organic brand with vanilla flavoring.

Just three days old. The little kittens lie nestled close to their mother's body or one of their siblings. Even though the babies have fur, at this age they can't keep their body temperature constant by themselves. Top photo: Isabella holds Sirena securely clasped in her front paws.

Middle photo: La Bomba lies tight on her mother's tummy and has drunk so much milk that she now sleeps full and happy next to her favorite nipple.

Bottom photo: Little Pauli has fallen asleep with one paw on mom's snout, and is dreaming open-mouthed after sucking milk.

Isabella and Serafina have done it. All the kittens have come into the world healthy.

Today at noon Isabella lies on the living room carpet and lets the sun shine on her belly. She is now seven weeks pregnant. All at once I see little, moving bulges inside her. The babies are pawing each other and remind me that it's time to set up a birthing place for the mother cat. Mother cats can be particular in this important matter, and may not take advice from us humans.

A Tailor-made Birthing Place

After lots of pacing back and forth, Serafina chooses the closet in my bedroom as a birthing place. I made a bottom shelf comfortable with a warm blanket and sheets. Isabella moves downstairs into the living room in a basket with a box over it. Cats like a cozy hole in a quiet place. Cats are looking for a comfortable environment with good access to the "restaurant." The mothers try out the future birthing places and dig around in the material to their satisfaction. My old male cat, Lionel, who loves all babies and helps raise them, sometimes takes his noonday snooze in there.

Meanwhile, we have fun betting on how many kittens there will be and what colors they will be. Mixed breed litters are always good for a surprise.

It's So Far, but Here I Am

A farm cat goes into the barn to give birth and hides the young in the straw. But cats that feel a close bond to their humans prefer to have loving company in those hours. The main thing is to radiate calm and give the cat a feeling of security. Any commotion or nervousness is only harmful.

At three o'clock that afternoon it's finally time. Isabella meows energetically for me to follow her to the birthing place. The necessary items are laid out in the room: a bowl of water, fresh sheets, and of course my veterinarian's phone number and a baby book. This baby book records the following: the time of birth, sex, number of afterbirths—which must always match the number of newborns—and finally, the weight of each kitten.

Amid serious labor pains, and with a piercing cry, Isabella gives birth to the first male cat, tail and hind legs first. This is not uncommon among cats, for around a third of them are born that way, rather than headfirst. Instinctively, Isabella opens the fetal envelope with her teeth, clears the little one's breathing passages with her coarse tongue, and licks him dry. Then she bites through the umbilical cord and eats the afterbirth (placenta).

The wild ancestors of our house cats used this instinctive behavior to keep the birthing place clean and take in crucial nutrients until they could once again go out hunting.

If the mother cat doesn't perform this important duty, you will have to help her out. Open up the fetal sac with your fingers and use a rough handkerchief to clean the mucous from the baby's nasal openings. Rub the fur dry against the lay of the hair; this stimulates the kitten's circulatory system.

La Bomba

THIS NIPPLE IS MINE

Every female cat has a total of eight nipples, plenty for six hungry babies. At least, one would think so. But usually there is a violent tussle over the hind "spigots." On the first day every kitten chooses its favorite nipple, which it recognizes by scent. And if necessary, it defends its nipple. Today as La Bomba is sucking contentedly on her number four, top row at the back, her brother Flori tries to barge in. There is an intense struggle with the forepaws. Both of them brace themselves firmly on the floor, but La Bomba doesn't let go. She wins, and Flori has to try someplace else.

The next youngsters are born in intervals of ten to fifty minutes. In the meantime, I stroke Isabella's body gently, talk to her in reassuring tones, and let her rest her hind legs against my hands through the labor pains. Once all six little ones are in the basket, I cover the area with a clean sheet. After that, Isabella is exhausted, but she lies contentedly on her side and purrs loudly while her babies nurse.

Serafina's delivery comes a couple of days later during the full moon. Since I had estimated a later delivery date, I'm not in place. Serafina gives me a good scolding and doesn't even give me time to have coffee. It's one o'clock in the morning, and she has waited for me long enough. Within an hour, five baby kittens are born—first the two strongest males, then two females, and finally one more male. They weigh between 3 and 4 ounces (90 and 110 g), all a little heavier than Isabella's little ones.

I really don't know who is happier about the offspring—the two mother cats or the people in the house. It doesn't matter; the main thing is that all are healthy and beautiful. A true gift.

The First Days

Serafina and Isabella leave their birthing places only to visit the litter box, drink, and get a small bite to eat in the evening. No wonder; anyone who has eaten that much high nutrition in the form of placenta gets filled up fast. Not so the little ones. They seem to have latched firmly on to Mom's filling station, in observance of the belief that whoever drinks the most will be the first one to

grow big. After all, a kitten must double its birth weight in the first week of life! The colostrum milk, which the mother cat produces in the first two days, contains important antibodies. They protect the offspring against infection over the next few weeks.

The little ones seem to like it, for they all lie close to one another, snuggling with full tummies in the nest. At night I sleep, accompanied by slurping, sucking noises, occasional quiet peeping, and Serafina's loud purring. It's a wonderful, meditative melody for sinking into sleep and having pleasant dreams.

Serafina tenderly licks her six-day-old kitten Bonita. Bonita is still blind and deaf, but her senses of touch and smell are so well developed that the youngster can recognize her mother from the first day.

The First Days

My granddaughter Jana is allowed to hold little Frederick very gently in her hand, and only on a cushion. With its 8 ounce (240 g) body weight, the fourteen-day-old male is still very fragile. And the little one's eyes have been open to the world for just a short while. But in the sensitive imprinting phase, loving skin contact with its human family is important.

Always on Call

When I watch my two mother cats, they remind me of people who work in emergency services. Even during dinner and through the night, these emergency helpers can be summoned on their pagers and immediately called to duty by peeping. Never mind that the two mothers are overflowing with milk and the little ones keep getting fatter; some still seem like they're not getting enough milk. One is Isabella's bluish-silver striped young-ster, a wonderful reflection of its mother. Only a delicate, yellowish-red spot on the forehead recalls their father Dolittle with his red coat.

At noon today as I serve Isabella a delicious meal and call her, the cat comes running to me with her tail happily held high. But who's that hanging from a nipple in the fur of her belly? And who plops onto the carpet and peeps so pitifully that Isabella immediately forgets her hunger and hurries to the scene? It's that greedy girl, whom I immediately christen Sirena. Her voice really is like a siren. And Sirena is the one, when all the other littermates are full and asleep together who switches on her peeping with such vehemence that Isabella immediately hurries back. Thank goodness. Sirena quiets down a little after about a week, precisely on the day when she becomes the first among all the little cats to open up her previously glued-shut eyelids and peer at the world with blue eyes.

The little kitten still can't see clearly, and she reacts negatively to bright light. Sirena is appar-ently overpowered by this new sensual stimulus. Mother Isabella can finally enjoy her hard-earned breaks.

Test:

Everything healthy and fully developed?

Yes	No	
○	○	1. Have all the kittens opened their eyes by at least the fourteenth day?
○	○	2. Do they regularly gain weight and lie full and happy in their nesting place?
○	○	3. Does the mother eat heartily several times a day, have good digestion, and maintain her weight to an acceptable degree?
○	○	4. Is the mother cat happy with her nesting place, not moving the little ones to other places?
○	○	5. At three weeks of age, can the little ones walk without their bellies touching the floor?
○	○	6. Starting in the second week, do the kittens react to noises in their surroundings?

Were you able to answer all questions with a definite yes? Great. Then everything is fine with your cat family. If not, I recommend you play it safe and consult your veterinarian.

Visitors Allowed?

Each cat is different, especially each mother cat. Many behave like furies when other cats come too close to their young ones. Even visits from two-legged creatures are tolerated only if they are from the immediate family. Other mother cats, on the other hand, march proudly through the house after just a few days and let the other residents visit the youngsters briefly. I always leave that choice to the mothers.

Isabella is the more concerned of the two and keeps a sharp eye out. If another cat spits at her little ones, it is immediately and energetically chased out of the room. Serafina, the female alpha cat of the house, acts like a queen. With a purred "It's all right," she lets all the other cats know visits are allowed. After dropping in, some of them lose interest. The two half-grown ones hiss somewhat halfheartedly, and then their curiosity seems satisfied.

Only my ten-year-old Maine Coon male, Sir Lionel, who has so far helped raise every litter,

At sixteen days, Sylvester is still so small that he can be held in both hands. Through our daily gentle touching sessions he has learned to trust his humans, and he recognizes us not only by smell, but also by our voices and shapes.

simply can't resist the baby cats. He waits respectfully, and only when the mothers pull back and purr their consent does he clamber into the nest among the little ones. At first I was afraid that the enormous Lionel, tipping the scales at 18 pounds (8 kg) would crush a kitten. But that never happens. With the utmost care he lies down around the babies, then takes them one after another in his enormous paws and licks them fervently. As with experienced mother cats, he first gives a tummy massage accompanied by licking the genital area of the little ones to stimulate elimination. And when the little one relieves itself, he licks it clean and eats the droppings. In these first weeks the kittens can't control their elimination by themselves, and they need this type of care. All my mother cats trust Lionel with their kittens and take advantage of the opportunity to catch up on their own hygiene.

Even though you are a proud and happy cat owner, you should hold back a little on visiting the cats in the first couple of weeks, especially if children in the house want to show their friends the sweet little kittens. The stress could be too much for the mother. It's always a good idea to take off your shoes every time you enter the house and wash your hands thoroughly with mild, unscented soap. However, it's not advisable to continually use disinfectant or antibacterial soap. As we know today, the immune system of

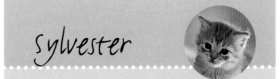

Sylvester

A SCENT TAKES CARE OF CONFUSION

Serafina's children are now six days old and still can't see or hear, but their senses of smell and touch work fine. They use scent to recognize their mother, Serafina, their favorite nipples, their littermates, and my trusted hands. They use their whiskers to perceive everything in their dark world. Today, as usual, as I speak to the cats and caress them lovingly, the little light red male cat hisses at me—he spits and hisses like a cobra. I smell my hand. New hand lotion? No. Have I touched a dog? No. Then it dawns on me. I prepared fish for lunch, and even though I have washed my hands, he can still smell it. Sorry, little Sylvester, soon you will be able to see and hear. Then you will recognize that your mistress is not a fish, but that fish is a tasty treat.

Isabella's kittens are now fourteen days old and look at the world through open eyes. Now their first milk teeth are appearing; they don't hurt the mother cat, though, since when the little ones suck milk, they latch onto the nipples with their tongues. Their ears are starting to stand up, and the little ones can now see and hear. Page 22: Firm in Isabella's grasp is little Sirena. Page 23: Sirena and her brother Flori.

healthy offspring needs a certain amount of training opportunities.

The First Tentative Steps

Today Flori took a tumble from a shelf in the closet, and I put down two cushions in front of the entryway to act as a bridge to the floor. That way the little ones can clamber in and out by themselves without danger.

Isabella's kittens, which are now almost three weeks old, are now padding around outside their basket. Sometimes just one kitten is left in the basket, and Isabella suckles the rest of the adventurers under the nearby radiator. I place flat trays of kitty

litter near both nests. The little ones make their way on wobbly legs to try it out. But the little cats don't know the first thing about how to begin.

The little ones mostly chew the litter. Many kittens do that, so use a nonclumping cat litter for the first six months. The first independent "business" seems to require lots of effort. The little one sits in the litter box and pushes hard until it's finally successful.

Even with the first cautious attempts at cleaning themselves, the kittens quickly lose their balance and fall over. But the world is waiting to be discovered as quickly as possible, with all senses and with their whole body.

Tip

Now the author's lactating cats are welcome to eat as much as they want four or five times a day. They get nutritious food (but not much dry food) such as cooked chicken, fish, lamb, and beef plus cottage cheese and vitamins every day.

Whee, Here I Come!

At three weeks the little kittens are padding around on wobbly legs. Now their movements are becoming quicker and more secure. Between the fourth and sixth weeks of life, the mother's milk is no longer adequate to satisfy the hunger of the active young ones. Now it's time for the little cats to try some solid food as well.

Playroom

WHEN THE KITTENS WERE BORN, their world was dark, quiet, and mysterious. They could feel the warmth and nearness of their littermates and the sudden coolness when they were left alone. They whimpered from hunger, and felt full and content after nursing. The baby cats explored their surroundings with their whiskers and learned to distinguish between the strange and the familiar by smell. Light and visual awareness entered their previously dark world between the seventh and twelfth day. And when their ears opened, the silence became filled with sounds and noises. These stimulating new senses mature between the fourth and fifth weeks, and are as well developed as a full-grown cat's.

Practice Makes Perfect

Until the little scamps achieve the physical dexterity and grace of the great softly padding hunters, they still have to practice and accumulate many experiences. The kittens are very curious, and are barely able to contain the impulse to explore. The adventuring can become stressful for a concerned mother cat. And for us devoted humans, too— you can't believe all the things kittens can get into. We'll talk more about that with my tips in the third chapter, and how this enthusiasm can be channeled into gentle and safe directions.

The needle-sharp milk teeth of the 5½-week-old kittens Felix and Sirena have left clear bite marks on the cardboard.

Weeks 4 through 6

Even Kittens Have to Learn How to Run

The way a kitten gets around in the first ten days reminds us of a seal on the beach. The nestling slides over the floor on its belly and pulls itself forward in the nest using paddling motions with its legs.

Only in the second week of life, when sight and hearing arrive on the scene, does the kitten succeed in standing more erect and maintaining its balance as it crawls forward. But it still walks clumsily as a plantigrade, with its whole paws planted flat on the floor. The tail, held perpetually stiff and high helps maintain balance.

Between the third and fourth week, the kitten begins to get around in the typical feline tiptoe stance. Its muscles can now support its entire body weight. But it still has to concentrate on its movements to maintain its balance and keep from falling over. Now the claws can be retracted and extended at will.

Between the fifth and sixth weeks of life, the kittens dash around in real cat fashion. Except when greeting other cats, they hold the tail low, with a slight outward bend at the end. The tail is no longer needed as a balancing aid in walking, but is now used as a steering mechanism in jumping. The leg movements have become more fluid and are no longer so awkward. The baby has turned into a child that imitates its mother in every way.

Watch Out, Two-Legged!

This morning I step out of the shower and reach for a towel. I feel something furry touch my foot. Instinctively I remain motionless and look down. My glance falls on a small bundle of fur cowering on the floor, ears laid back and big blue eyes looking at me in alarm. As I bend over the kitten, a few drops of water have the great misfortune to fall from my wet hair onto the kitten's fur. That's too much of a good thing. The pound and a half (700 g) of scared kitten rushes off like a shot. The legs scarcely seem to touch the floor.

Sirena's retreat doesn't stop until she reaches her mother, Isabella, in the basket. Isabella licks her kitten solicitously and gives Sirena an extra ration of milk. The kitten slowly falls asleep amid purring, snuggled close to her mother's warm body. I'm glad nothing serious happened.

Living with Giants

When kittens discover their world between the fourth and sixth weeks of life, they are about 6½ inches (17 cm) high. But we bipeds walk around with an average height of 5 feet, 7 inches (170 cm). Thus, if we were kittens, on a corresponding scale of one to ten, we would be living with giants 53 feet (17 m) tall. That's about as tall as a two-story apartment building! That's a frightening concept.

Another consideration for kittens is that we giants often forget what's happening on the floor going on between our feet. Mother cats watch out carefully for their offspring, for the babies are not familiar with many dangers. We have to watch out for the little ones and look down before we sit down.

Despite decades of experience raising cats, I am always amazed at what the little ones can

Frederick

A COURAGEOUS CAT?

Right from the beginning, he was sensitive: gentle and dependent. At the age of four weeks, when Frederick saw his first live mouse, which had just crawled brazenly over his head, he lost all his macho courage. He cowered, drew his ears back, and slunk away. Has he forgotten that he is the hunter and that the mouse is the prey? It's good that later on he can play the role that fits him best: a gentle cuddler that preys only on toy mice.

get into through their urge to explore. On pages 34, 36, 37, and 39 I describe what a house that's safe for cats is like.

Playing Develops the Mind

Did you know that a long, sheltered childhood with lots of time for playing makes kittens more intelligent? In a protected setting, playing provides experience and physical training. Playing is not a waste of time, but a biologically useful exercise.

"Good grief, what's that?" Little Frederick seems not to understand his four-week-old cat world. He already knows other cats, and some rare two-leggeds as well. But Mommy Serafina has yet to show him what cats do with an audacious little mouse.

Playful romping with siblings is now the order of the day. And with kittens, there is no dictum like the common statement "Girls don't do such things." Female kittens are allowed to be as wild and daredevilish as male cats. At six weeks, the young scamps usually are not quite as wild as they are a few weeks later, for the kittens still have to develop their physical abilities.

Photos top and middle: Bonita launches an attack from above on Sylvester, who defends himself. He loses his balance and tips to the side.

Lower photo: The kitten Sylvester romps with his brother Frederick.

From the fourth week on, a kitten prefers to play with other kittens, or with Mom's tail.

Of course, a kitten doesn't have to learn everything, for it has already inherited instinctual knowledge from its forebears and does the right thing. The blind, deaf baby cat thus finds its mother's teat without help and knows how to suck the life-giving milk from it, and how to stimulate the milk-producing glands by kneading with its forepaws. Later on, the kitten can purr, spit, and use other feline vocalizations without having to go through the tedious process of learning them. Other behaviors are learned through personal experience with the surroundings, observation, and through instruction from the mother cat. Physical abilities and dexterity, which now increase weekly, must be developed further through daily practice. But, kittens are good learners.

Starting around the fourth week, kittens begin to play. At first, the littermates are pawed tentatively, but soon it turns into a regular tussle. By the fifth week the senses are fully developed, but the little ones still need serious training of their physical abilities. Therefore, social play among the kittens and with their mother moves to center stage. Starting with the seventh week, purposeful play involving prey becomes interesting. The little rascals turn into increasingly skillful hunters.

Sometimes It's Hard Being a Mom

Poor Serafina. The kittens are becoming increasingly active, and they resist being reined in. Instead of staying upstairs and behaving, Sylvester in particular runs up and down the corridor and hops down the stairs. But now the game is over! Serafina grabs the mischief-maker by the scruff of the neck and drags him back into the safety of the room. But at five weeks the male cat has become so big and heavy she can hardly drag him up the steps. Thump, thump, thump it goes—held motionless in his mother's mouth in the "limp response" as his bottom bumps on every step. Scarcely has Serafina recovered from the effort and lovingly licked the little rascal, when the game starts all over again. Now the mother uses a forceful, hissed reprimand, and if that doesn't do the trick, a blow with the paw. Still, Serafina's patience seems boundless.

But suddenly she's fed up with all the schlepping and becomes the watchful and solicitous companion on the expeditions of her adventurous children. Perhaps she also relies on my human guardianship as the top cat. Outdoors, alone in a dangerous environment, she would supervise her band of offspring more energetically and hustle them back into the secure nest. This measure can be a lifesaver in case an enemy suddenly appears. And even the young ones

Serafina now suckles her young ones in shifts: sometimes two, sometimes three, and if one like Sylvester should come in late, he gets a separate serving. Tail held high, a licking of the fur, an exchange of family scent, and Sylvester is ready to take off again. Serafina has him tight in her grasp. The milk bar is first opened when Mom is ready.

couldn't allow themselves to romp around in such a carefree manner.

But my two mother cats need lots of patience when they become pieces of gymnastics equipment, or are recruited for the game of Catch Mom's Tail. Fortunately, in both rooms there are bureaus the mothers can climb onto to get some rest. The little rogues still have many weeks to grow and exercise before they become able to follow them onto these lofty heights.

Little Behavior Studies

When kittens begin to discover their surroundings, it is a joy to observe. It is also funny, exciting, and informative to watch them. Until the

little ones become independent and leave the house at around three months, there is intense communication among the kittens, and between the mother cat and her young ones. The kittens' development at this time is unlike any other life stage, with a tremendous variety of behaviors. Take advantage of this opportunity and spend as much time as possible with your companion animals. That way you will learn to understand cats and lay the groundwork for a happy and rewarding life together.

The Greeting Ritual

When cats live under the care of humans, and especially when they are kept indoors, they are oriented to our care and the food we provide.

Tip

Learn to understand "catish" by observing. And as a giant to your cats, develop a greeting ritual in which you lie flat on the floor and coax them to you in a friendly manner.

A Safe Playground for Kittens

1 **ELECTRICAL WIRES:** Remove wiring, place it high and out of reach, or hide it inside conduit. When they're teething, kittens like to chew wiring, and they can receive a fatal electrical shock.

2 **RUBBER BANDS, THREADS, AND STRING:** Never leave such things lying around. In playing, a kitten can choke on them or experience a dangerous intestinal blockage if it swallows them. Cat toys attached to string or elastic should be used only with supervision and put away promptly afterward.

3 **OPPORTUNITIES FOR SCRATCHING:** A board secured to the wall at an angle, measuring about eight by twenty-four inches (20 × 60 cm) and covered with sisal or coconut fiber, belongs in every cat room right from the beginning. An additional scratching and climbing tree covered with hemp or sisal and with a napping spot on top also serves as fitness apparatus.

4 **CAT GRASS:** This is especially helpful to long-haired cats in vomiting up hair ingested through grooming. Fresh green oats and wheat are ideal. Pay close attention with cypress grass to be sure the edges are not too sharp; otherwise they could hurt mucous membranes. My cats are very fond of nibbling indoor bamboo.

5 **HIDING PLACES:** Solid cardboard boxes of any size, open or closed on top, with openings cut on the sides, are great stimulators for playing hide-and-seek with littermates.

6 **REMOVE FROM THE ROOM** anything that can be broken or swallowed, or that can be toxic to cats, such as certain houseplants. Be careful with recesses behind dressers, entertainment centers, or bookshelves, for the little rascals can fall into them and get stuck.

Free-ranging cats and mousers live less comfortably, but to a certain degree they are more independent. These very different lifestyles also determine the attitude of grown cats toward humans. Behavioral science tells us that a subordinate cat behaves with us two-leggeds as a kitten does with its mother. To our cats, we are sort of two-legged, alpha mother cats from which they seek attention. They snuggle up to us and expect our hands to stroke them like huge tongues. And even the stiff, erect tails when cats come running to us is a typical greeting ritual that kittens use with their mothers. It is also an invitation to inspect the anal area.

A friendly greeting is more than a way to get attention, though. It's also a means to exchange scents that strengthen the family group. So when a cat rubs against its human, it is marking the person with its scent, which means, "I like you. You belong to me." This exchange of scents, which our human noses cannot detect, takes place with the help of scent glands in the cat's chin, lips, and cheeks. If the cat ever has the opportunity to reach our faces, for example, when we lie with it on a sofa, bed, or on the floor, it can greet us in typical cat fashion: it rubs its nose against ours, rubs us with its head, and walks up and down in front of us with its hindquarters, and tail held high so we can inspect its anal region.

Please don't be put off by this or regard it as repulsive; it's a sign of affection on the part of your four-legged friend. The much smaller cat often has to make do with what it can reach on us big two-leggeds. So it rubs its sides against our legs, swings its tail around, and looks up expectantly to our faraway heads, where the friendly

Early on, the kittens practice to see who is going to be a good climber and master claw sharpener. For Flori, six weeks old, a climbing tree only 32 inches (80 cm) high is a good idea, since there is still a problem getting down safely.

voices come from. It attempts a stiff-legged hop, skip, and jump by way of a greeting, and then happily presses its head against our hand when finally it is lowered to pet it lovingly. And how it purrs and kneads with its paws, when the sounds of meal preparation ring out. "Finally, my human is back. Soon I will be fed. Wonderful!"

Sirena

A PHONE CONVERSATION WITH CONSEQUENCES

Just as I was taking the litter box out of Isabella's kitty room for cleaning, the phone rang. My best friend was on the line, and we talked for a long time. Almost two hours later I brought the cleaned litter box back into the room. Oh, no! All my notes, which I had written lying on the floor with the cats, had been ransacked. Nearly every page was embellished by a chewed-off corner, and Sirena was staring around busily. She has a well-developed sense of priorities. Her little "ocean" landed not on the everyday rug, but right on the important notes.

A Room for the Mob

It can be a real hassle to make every room in the house cat-proof. Especially if you have to leave the mob without supervision, it's comforting to know it's good and safe. A playroom set aside for the kittens helps with housebreaking, prevents bad habits, and facilitates safe play, at least until the little ones have learned the most important things. In a house where there is more than one cat, it also allows the mother cat to get a break and gives her a sense of security. And it's a place where the important supplementary food can be put out without all other four-leggeds running in to gobble it up.

I had a door specially built with a bottom half made of Plexiglas and the upper half made of wire mesh. For temporary accommodations for the offspring, though, a wire or plastic barrier for children that spans the door frame is adequate. So that no kittens can squeeze through the openings in the mesh, cover it with a clear Plexiglas sheet, because the little ones would chew through a net or use it to climb over. This keeps the kittens in visual contact with what's going on outside and is not as isolating as keeping them behind a closed door.

When you set up a room, take into account the advice on page 34. If the window opens outward for ventilation, the opening must be closed up with a screen. If a window has to be kept wide open in the summer, it is best blocked off with a

When the kittens attempted their first grooming, they lost their balance and fell down. Now, at five weeks, the kitten Sylvester has mastered the ritual, and just like his mom, he licks his forepaw and uses it to wash his face.

metal screen with openings measuring ¾ × 1.5 inches (20 × 40 mm) with wire about .025 inch (0.7 mm) thick. Kittens will quickly chew through plastic cat mesh. The cat room should also have two ceramic bowls that keep the water cool and fresh. For feeding the kittens and the mother you will need three large, shallow bowls set up an adequate distance from the litter box. Cats are sensitive to odors and, like people, don't like to eat next to the toilet.

For the mother cats, place their accustomed litter box in a peaceful corner of the room. An open plastic litter box is a good choice or, as in my house, a litter box with a cover that keeps the cats from scratching the litter out of the box.

Housebreaking Made Easy

As already described in the first chapter, housebreaking begins when the kittens are three to four weeks old. Pet supply stores sell special low litter boxes for kittens. This makes it possible for even the littlest kittens to climb in without difficulty. The mother cat usually stops cleaning up after her kittens when the young ones start eating solid food at four to six weeks. Because the kittens don't wander far from their nest at the beginning, their litter box should be set up close to their basket. Usually the young ones learn through play and curiosity to go in, and they are

The six-week-old male kitten Felix cheerfully "speaks" to his human friend by treading with his forepaws in the air, and appears to enjoy being stroked. Lying relaxed in a person's arms and displaying its belly is a sign of great trust.

quick to understand that the litter is not to eat, but rather to use for a toilet. Cleaning the litter box several times a day is a must at this point, for otherwise the kittens will look for a cleaner alternative someplace in the room.

If there should be a mishap at the beginning in spite of everything, clean it up immediately and thoroughly using a hand soap with an orange oil additive. Don't use any cleaning products that contain ammonia; because of the similarity of the odor to urine, it would only further stimulate your cat to urinate in the same place. And don't lose your cool if an accident happens. Your kittens are still babies. Anyone who yells, shoves the cat's nose into its business, or roughly pushes it back into the litter box accomplishes nothing more than frightening the kitten and encourages it to search for a secretive place.

Successful training requires praise and rewards. When the kitten succeeds in doing its business in the litter box, stroke it a moment and speak to it with friendly words: "You did very well." The cat likely doesn't understand the words you say to it. But it perceives your positive emotions and will associate the litter box with good feelings.

At Mom's Milk Bar

When mother cats, like mine, are given nutritious food, they suckle their young ones for up to three months. And many a lazy rascal takes his sweet time trying different types of food. A mother cat has to help out by making it clear from that point on that the faucet is turned off. But that hasn't occurred yet. Several times a day Isabella and

Serafina purr, call their young ones together, and lie down on their sides to suckle them. The little ones slurp as they hang on to the teats and simultaneously massage the mother's belly with rhythmic treading to stimulate the milk glands and encourage the flow. This so-called "milk

kneading" is instinctive and continues into adulthood. When a grown cat is petted, for example, and kneads your lap, it seems to recall its youth. In any case, the kneading is always an expression of contentment.

From Mother's Milk to Other Treats

A free-ranging barnyard cat brings dead prey animals to its offspring as early as four weeks after birth, and the little ones chew on it. A few weeks later there is a demonstration using live prey.

Even when the mother cat's milk is still flowing freely, offer the young ones some supplementary food starting in the fourth or fifth week. Usually appetite occurs naturally, and kittens learn to eat out of curiosity when Mom eats it first. For practice you can serve the kitten a little yogurt or cream on your finger so it can learn to lick instead of sucking. It's a good idea to have three ceramic bowls with a 1 inch (2.5 cm) rim and about 7 inches (19 cm) in diameter. These make a common meal possible and are not easy to tip over.

Suggested menu and feeding routine: feed three to four times a day, alternating between cream cheese with raw egg yolk and warm water whisked in, cottage cheese, and mild yogurt. Later you can add canned food for kittens, small bits of cooked chicken, or cooked fish fillet. It it not possible to give exact quantities. Offer as much as the kittens will eat within a twenty-minute period.

Flori

BON APPÉTIT!

Isabella is still suckling her young ones tirelessly. But at the age of five weeks, and with so much tussling, the youngsters are using up so much energy that supplemental food is called for. But that's easier said than slurped. So far the mother's milk has been sucked from a teat. How do you suck up milk from a bowl? Flori has already learned to lick yogurt from a finger. But it's hilarious when he sticks his whole snout in and plugs up his nostrils. Don't be so impetuous, little Flori. Just use your tongue like a soup spoon and things will work better.

Yum, yum—delicious cream cheese with egg yolk stirred in sure is good. Flori licks his chops while his two 5½-week-old siblings continue eating heartily.

Thereafter, wash the bowls with hot water; don't leave any food in the bowls or offer any more. Everything has to be provided fresh, but not straight from the refrigerator. This can cause problems with the stomach and digestion.

The Socialization Phase

This segment of development is also called the "sensitive stage." With kittens it begins at the age of two weeks and concludes at around twelve

The hat may be too big for the head, but the kitten can still hide under it, even if the behind doesn't fit in. Lying on her back, La Bomba invites us to come play with her when she stretches out on the floor and then happily kneads the air with her paws. Hiding under the hat and sticking out the paws is typical cat behavior. You just never know when a mouse will pass by.

weeks. In that time it's decided whether the kitten will turn into a cuddly, devoted family cat, or will regard us as creatures that are better avoided. Many kittens that go through this important socialization phase without loving human contact will be shy and distrustful of us. It takes endless patience and empathy to win their trust. And anyone who wants a cat that gets along with other cats should make sure that the cat grows up in a group of well-socialized cats.

Both socialization phases generally occur independently of each other. So a young cat will not become especially dependent on humans if it is taken away from its mother and siblings as early as possible. The best age for getting a kitten is between twelve and fourteen weeks; at that

point the whole litter should already be wormed and vaccinated.

You Don't Understand Me

Today my friend Brigitte and her daughter Susie come to visit the sweet little cats. There is plenty of excitement. We adults aren't paying close attention, and Susie drags the cats around, holds them tight to her, and stuffs them into the doll carriage. Suddenly all the little ones have disappeared under the bureaus. "Aunt Monika, they don't want to play anymore!" Right! It's a wonder that none of the cats scratched her. I suggest a role play, which Susie gladly accepts. Susie is to play kitten, crawl around on all fours, meow, lick her paws,

Tip

Indoor only cats are wormed for the first time at six weeks, and for the second time at ten weeks. Free-ranging cats need more thorough worming. Discuss this subject with your veterinarian.

curl up, and sleep. I take on the role of the child: I run yelling through all the rooms dragging "Susie the kitten" behind. I pull her around, and don't let go unless I want to. I tickle her and pet her every-where. And suddenly I shove Susie into bed against her will. At some point Susie ceases to find the game amusing: "Phooey, this is a stupid game!" Right! But it worked. And now I can explain to the attentive Susie what cats love and what they really don't like. At the end of the day,

Susie lies peacefully on the floor and all the kittens play confidently around her.

Hello, My Name Is . . .

When I call my kittens to me, in a coaxing tone of voice, by saying, "Kitties, come eat!" they all come running with tails held high. The tone of voice makes the music. Still, every kitten should have its own name, which will accompany it when it's

Flashing her typical baby blue eyes, five-week-old Sirena charms the camera from under her blanket. In the coming weeks her eyes will get more pigmentation until they take on the beautiful amber color of her mother Isabella's eyes.

handed over to its new family. Often this naming takes place spontaneously. With other animals, it takes longer to decide; people ask friends and acquaintances, or look in an appropriate book of names.

I had to name a total of eleven kittens, including five superstars. So Isabella's kids were called Flori, Felix, and Pipo for the males, and Sirena, La Bomba, and Little Pauli for the females. For Serafina's litter: Sylvester, Amadeus, Frederick, and Pascha for the males, and Bonita for the female. The story of how La Bomba came to have her name is related on this page. Sirena was named spontaneously for her voice (see page 19). Later she spoke to us with a magical little voice, and that too is fitting. Like the sirens who tried to lead Odysseus astray, she has her own charm as a sweet cat princess.

I named Flori after the son of a friend. And like him, Flori turned into a snack gobbler, so I had to put him on a low-cal diet of half rations at the age of seven months. Charming Sylvester, our champion cat, puts people in a good mood just like a glass of champagne on New Year's Eve. Frederick got his name from a mouse with the same name, the hero of a famous children's book. So how surprising was it that later on he was no great mouser? Felix the happy was not singled out to be a superstar. But later he provided his human family with so much happiness that he more than lived up to his name.

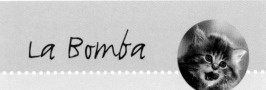

La Bomba

THE LITTLE STAR

"Oh, how sweet!" everyone remarks when the fluffy little kitten runs up to them. And the little one greets every visitor with the same unreserved joy. "Bombastico," I say when she acts in front of the camera. "Oh, là là," I say whenever she surprises us with one of her spontaneous actions. Maybe it's because this summer I have spent too much time in my favorite Italian restaurant; in any case, this kitten gets the name La Bomba. Her mother, Isabella is not Italian, for she is a purebred Brit: in fact, a British Shorthair, blue-silver tabby in color. La Bomba's dad, who is named Dolittle, is a mixture of Persian and Maine Coon. With so much ethnic diversity, La Bomba was sure to make a real splash and become a versatile and beloved star.

Fit for Fun

At the age of **seven to nine weeks** the kittens begin practicing—playfully, but with great enthusiasm and increasing skill—for their eventual roles as hunters, predators, and fighters. But in the meantime the little warriors lovingly groom their fur and sleep cuddled together.

Little Hunters ...

SOMEWHERE AROUND THE SEVENTH WEEK the kittens concentrate on their later role as hunters. Unfortunately—or thank goodness—no mice are scurrying around in my house, and no birds are fluttering through the air. Only occasionally in the winter, when it's really cold, does a frozen and half-starved rodent stray into my attic, which borders the old barn on the farm. And then we humans are reminded that a wild hunter still slumbers inside our relaxed, cuddly couch tigers. Even in the summer, when all kinds of insects such as flies, gnats, and moths stray through open windows and doors, they are all hunted down and gobbled up. And what my kittens lack in experience they make up for in redoubled enthusiasm for the hunt and physical effort. The little ones turn out to be aerial acrobats by following the motto "If the prey flies, I fly after it."

The Kittens' Favorite Games

There seems to be no limit to their fantasy; the clowder* turns into prey anything that crosses their path, and every kitten shows marked preferences.

La Bomba loves marbles best, which she drags into the bathtub. There she lies on the edge of the tub and bats the marbles up and down the

La Bomba celebrates Mardi Gras with us, catches colorful paper streamers, and excitedly lurks in the tangle for new prey.

Weeks 7 through 9

tub walls with her paws; many times it seems that she has more than four of them. The more noise they make, the better. The racket makes me think that laborers are in my house.

Yesterday Flori stole from a box some little soft pieces that were used as packing material and played with them in the living room. Fortunately, the material was made of natural materials. I would have had to take away Styrofoam or other synthetics, which could cause serious problems with the stomach and digestion if swallowed. Styrofoam and similar materials must be kept away from kittens and cats. They can also cause intestinal blockages, requiring surgery.

Sirena prefers to play with a toy mouse that has a built-in microchip. When it is thrown up in the air or bumped, it squeaks like a live mouse. Sirena finds that amusing. Sylvester and Frederick show themselves to be aerial acrobats when I throw Ping-Pong balls so they bounce off the wall or the floor. The two of them race after the ball and try to bat it out of the air with their paws.

They all have fun with the "cat rod," on the end of which is a piece of feather hanging from a length of elastic. In the evening before feeding the cats, I take it out and wave it around in front of them so they get the impression a bird is flying around. Whoever manages to catch the "bird" runs away with the rod and the elastic.

*Pack of dogs, clowder of cats.

At eight weeks Flori has learned to leap from one chair to another on command. He pushes off with his powerful hind legs and stretches out his body, with his front paws drawn in. To cushion the shock and land safely, he first plants his now extended forelegs, and then the hind legs, which are now held closer to the body. Cats have an outstanding sense of balance and a tail that functions as a rudder.

Usually the kitten and its prey disappear under a bureau. From that point on, the kitten purrs and defends the prey against all rivals. It's important for a cat to experience this success in hunting; otherwise it will lose interest in it. After a while, you can distract the little predator and make the bird fly again. Never grab the prey away forcefully. The kitten could sustain an injury to the mouth or have a claw pulled out. Indoor cats need plenty of chances to play and keep busy. Learning tasks that are fun for the owner and the animal foster not only the kitten's faculties and skills, but also its attachment to its human.

Come and Jump to Me!

Here you can see how I train my photo model to jump on command. At around eight weeks the

kitten has the physical agility to master the following exercise. The prerequisite for this is that the kitten has already learned to come to you when it's called.

You will need two sturdy stools with non-slip surfaces of wicker or fabric. They must not wiggle, tip over, or be too slippery, or the kitten will not feel secure. At first, place the stools about 20 inches (50 cm) apart. This short distance will be easy for the kitten to handle. Train one cat at a time to reduce distractions. Take one of the cat's favorite treats. This can be a cat snack, a little piece of turkey ham, or anything that your cat particularly likes. Now crouch behind a stool and lure the kitten onto the stool with the command, "Yummy, a treat. Jump!" When it hops up, pat the kitten, praise it, and give it a reward.

Repeat as many times as necessary for the cat to catch on. Obviously, this exercise is practiced before meals and without a full stomach, since couch tigers that have had enough to eat prefer to relax. When the cat is perched on the stool, crouch behind the facing stool and lure the cat

Sirena

AN UNSUCCESSFUL LESSON

Isabella meows loudly to call her young ones together. Most are romping upstairs in the loft and don't hear a thing, but Sirena rushes in. What does Mom have in her mouth? Oh, it's a mouse! Isabella lets the prey go and bats it with her paw. Sirena sniffs it and looks on in amazement. And now Isabella is following her instinct and wants to share a lesson with her offspring. Little Sirena momentarily finds the toy mouse boring and flies up the stairs to her siblings. Who knows? Maybe there is a real mouse hidden up there.

with an enticing tone of voice. Put a little excitement into your voice. You can also wave the cat rod (see page 49).

Next, slightly increase the length of the jump once the kitten has completed the task successfully. Crafty or lazy cats often try to land on the floor between the stools, rather than jumping all the way between them. In that case, say, "No!" firmly, and of course, give no reward.

In any case, don't train the animal for more than about ten minutes at a stretch, and don't increase the degree of difficulty too quickly. All exercises should provide fun and be done playfully. If the cat loses interest and goes away, accept it. Cats can be passionately engaged in a task, but if they find it boring, away they go. The same is true for my cat photography, and when I'm training cats for a film. Cats are not dogs that happily and tirelessly repeat the mistress's exercises.

Who's the Boss Around Here?

The tussling among littermates keeps getting wilder, and sometimes they cross the boundary between playful and serious. One kitten will stalk another, with its body low to the floor. The tip of the tail flicks back and forth in excitement. Then come the leap and the attack on the other cat, preferably from cover, and the kitten lands on its opponent's back. The victim usually rolls lightning-fast onto its back so it can use powerful thrusts from its hind legs to defend itself from the attacker. Both combatants now tussle and bite each other's ears. Angry stares, spitting, and laid-back ears are signals that one of the two no longer find the game so amusing. If it runs away,

there may be a wild pursuit through all the rooms that the other cats take up spontaneously.

Sometimes it's no longer possible to figure out who is fighting with or chasing whom, for the game can change quickly. Still, these tussles usually don't lead to real injuries. Any that has had enough can withdraw to an elevated lookout. From there it looks out over the play of the others, until it plunges back into the fray with a new sneak attack. A kitten continually tries to make a big impression on its opponent. It stands stiff-legged on tiptoes, arches its back, and fluffs up

Flori and Felix are tired from the wild rumble and have fallen asleep cuddled together. As they were having their tummies gently rubbed, they stretched out all four legs, and they now purr a duet as they dream.

What Kittens Can Do

HOUSEBREAKING: All kittens are dependably clean. Between weeks four and five they learn to use their kitten litter boxes. Now they scratch enthusiastically in the high, roomy litter boxes for adult cats that are distributed all around the house (see p. 88).

CLIMBING: Every day the kittens can develop their skills on low scratching and climbing trees. Now they have learned you don't climb down head-first, but rather with the hind legs first. That's the only way that the inward curving claws provide a hold and prevent a fall.

EATING INDEPENDENTLY: Even if the little ones are still allowed to suckle mother's milk, they are no longer dependent on it. They could grow up on the food that's provided three to four times a day.

THE POSITION OR TURNING REFLEX: If a cat falls some distance, even if the cat is upside down to begin with, it still lands on all four feet. The astonishing ability to turn into the correct landing position during a free fall is developed as early as the sixth week.

HUNTING SKILLS: Everything that moves and can be caught is regarded as prey. Preparations for hunting include playful stalking, pouncing, biting, tossing, and carrying "mice." A toy attached to a string becomes a bird that can be jumped for and caught in the air.

PLAY OR SERIOUSNESS: The catching and attacking games, and the pursuits and tussles among littermates, become increasingly refined. The overall repertoire of behavior becomes more playful and conversely often more serious, including such things as dominating, threatening, submitting, and attacking.

the fur on its back and tail so the tail looks like a bottlebrush.

Then it dances sideways toward its opponent like a young colt. Next follows a new attack; both combatants pounce on each other and tumble wildly around the room. Only when the warriors tire do they retreat to a quiet place—some on their own, and others cuddled together. Then they are all once again at peace, for everything is play for the little predators.

The First Shots

All the mothers of my kittens have, of course, had their shots, so the little ones already have some antibodies in their blood at birth to help protect them against life-threatening diseases. In the womb, the antibodies are transferred to the babies through the female cat's blood, and later on it is passed on to the young ones through what's known as colostrum milk (page 17). At around eight weeks, this protection loses its effectiveness, and so my veterinarian is coming to the house today to inoculate all eleven kittens against the most dangerous infectious diseases. That's no easy task with these whirlwinds,, which jump around like a sac of fleas.

To make things go quicker, I stroke the little patient, and distract the kitten by offering a special treat. Two little pinpricks and it's all over. The veterinarian injects a combination of vaccines for cat distemper (panleukopenia) and feline respiratory disease (rhinotracheitis); the second injection supplies the vaccine for feline leukemia.

Depending on temperament, sensitivity to pain, and even on how the kittens feel on a given

La Bomba has mastered washing herself as perfectly as a grown-up cat. And since she has been lapping up cream, she now cleans her fur with special care.

day, some of them appear not to notice anything, and others squeal loudly. That's what happens with our charming macho Sylvester and the little princess Sirena, whereas the even-tempered Flori takes everything in stride, in accordance with his temperament.

The same applies to the reactions to the shots. Within the next twenty-four hours, most of the kittens need to rest, and several eat with reduced appetite for a short time. That is normal, and it goes away. After three to four weeks the little ones are inoculated for a second time. Kittens that later will be allowed to roam free must also be inoculated against rabies. Then all shots are renewed yearly.

Finding the Right Veterinarian

I am very happy that my cat family is treated by an experienced and personable veterinarian who is a cat owner himself. Further pluses are that he makes house calls on request and offers emergency services.

Climbing up and down a tree trunk is no problem for the 8½-week-old Sylvester. The kitten can also sharpen his claws nicely on the wood and simultaneously mark his climbing tree.

Here are some recommendations for finding a good veterinarian, which will help you become acquainted and develop a mutual trust. All of a sudden your beloved cat needs medical care.

How to find it? Ask other cat owners about their experiences, and inquire at local pet supply stores to get recommendations for good veterinarians.

Location: The clinic should be within a reasonable distance; it's important to be able to reach your veterinarian quickly. In an emergency situation, it can make a life or death difference if the clinic is within fifteen minutes, as opposed to fifty.

➤ Appointment times: I don't appreciate it when I make an appointment for my cat, show up on time, and then have to wait in the clinic with my sick animal for an hour or more. This should happen only when an unforeseen emergency, which of course takes precedence, disrupts the schedule.

➤ Service: A house call can be important if you can't go to the clinic yourself, the animal is too ill and would be stressed by travel and transport, or you have several cats. Is the veterinarian willing to make house calls? Another plus is emergency veterinarian service on weekends and holidays. That may save you a trip to an animal clinic where no one knows your cat's medical history and you may have to provide lengthy explanations.

➤ Ask for demonstrations: Every cat owner starts as a beginner, and there are plenty of things you may know but not be able to do on the first try.

Frederick

SUCCESSFUL HUNTING

My friend and I are cuddling on the sofa and relaxing with a glass of red wine on a Saturday night and watching the kittens play. Suddenly all hell breaks loose. All the cats are jumping over the furniture and up the walls, chattering excitedly. Before we grasp what has happened, one of the frenetic predators pounces on the living room lamp, and the wineglasses fall over. But that's not all: with one of the cats in the lead, and the whole group behind it, they all run up the stairs. We find them all assembled upstairs. They crouch in a semicircle around the bureau, from under which emanate some frightful noises. I lie flat on my stomach and look underneath. There lurks Frederick with a moth in his mouth; he growls, claws unsheathed, ready to prevent anyone from taking his prey. Yes, Frederick, now you have become a real hunter. I only hope that you liked the taste of the moth.

Who says that I am always the good-natured little Flori? At nine weeks I can catch prey, and I am ready for any kind of wild game.

Here's how these photos came about: Flori was hunting and had hidden behind a small table. My assistant moved a rod with a tuft of feathers attached to it under the edge of the tablecloth, much like a mouse running through dense leaves. Flori's response was a blow with the paw with sharp claws extended, the whiskers forward, and a quick peek over the edge. "I've got that mouse!" Flori's gaze is wild, and his bite to the prey leaves no doubt that there is no escape for the "mouse."

Cats want to be respected and understood.
They react to any kind of force with protest.

Don't be shy about asking your veterinarian to explain and show you how to perform important tasks like taking a temperature and giving medications.

➤ Ask questions. Veterinarians are not gods, but ideally helpful partners for your pet's care. To the extent possible, find out about the options, treatments, and costs. That builds knowledge and trust, and avoids frustration later on.

➤ Support: The more support you provide, the better the veterinarian can help your pet. If your cat becomes ill, write down when the first symptoms occurred, such as loss of appetite, apathy, vomiting, and diarrhea. How did your cat's behavior change? Bring along the vaccination record, if the doctor did not give the vaccinations him- or herself. Always transport your cat in a secure, protective carrier.

➤ Interpersonal relationships: A veterinarian should always use a friendly tone and demeanor. The veterinarian must deal with stress well, because when a pet is sick, injured, and in a state of panic, the pet owner may react the same way out of concern for their friend. Don't forget to compliment your veterinarian and offer thanks for a job well done after a successful and gentle treatment.

Important Rules of Conduct

Cats are animated, worthy, and sensitive creatures. Many people are fascinated by these enig-matic beings; others don't care for cats because they seem to be aloof and disloyal. People who don't like cats may have a problem with the fact that cats always maintain a measure of independence, even though they accept food and attention from us humans. They are not like dogs that are pack animals and try to please the leader of the pack, whether master or mistress. Cats react with protest to any kind of force and can develop so-called "behavior disorders," but the true disorder usually lies in our human lack of understanding and the resulting unseemly behavior.

Please Do Not Disturb!

Practice calmness and tolerance. This doesn't mean that you shouldn't train your cat. Just do it gently, as with a firm "No!" when it does something it shouldn't. It involves keeping a watchful eye and sensing the cat's nature and needs. For example, no cat likes to be overwhelmed with petting against its will, or to be grabbed forcefully and carried around. And when a cat is eating, taking a midday snooze, or grooming itself intensively, it doesn't want to be disturbed. You have to learn to accept these basic conditions.

Learn to Wait!

A cat comes to its human when it is ready, and not always when we want it to. I admit, this is not always easy to accept, especially when we ardently want this wonderfully cuddly, purring creature on our lap so we can pet it. But patience with our cats helps us become more respectful and tolerant of other people and their differences.

In the last twenty years I have noticed that men who get along well with cats are also more understanding of women. That doesn't mean, of course, that male cat lovers necessarily understand women better; they simply are more tolerant. This thesis has also not been proven scientifically, but in my view it would merit a more thorough study.

Quiet, Please!

Eliminate the stress: That's the motto of all cats. Lots of hubbub around them—yelling, loud music especially in high frequencies, arguing, and unpleasant noises such as slamming doors—go against their grain. Cats like a quiet but stimulating environment.

Changes? No, Thanks!

Cats are creatures of habit. They like regular and prompt times for feeding, playing, and cuddling. People who continually move furniture and cat fixtures around bring no joy into the heart of any cat. Moving to a new residence is another cause of stress for your pet. Strangers should always be polite and introduce themselves to the cat. This is best done in a crouch, approximately at eye level with the cat; the cat is allowed to sniff the back of the slightly outstretched hand as they speak to the animal with a friendly, calm voice. Then they should wait until the cat comes closer to them of its own accord.

Picking Up and Carrying the Right Way

If you want to pick up a cat, take it slow and carefully. Never grab the animal from behind unprepared, and don't startle it out of sleep. When you pick up a cat, hold it with one hand

Flori

OH NO, HE GOT IN . . .

On baking day the kitchen door is always kept shut because I don't need lots of cats zooming around between my feet. When I'm in the middle of kneading the dough, my cell phone on the cupboard in the corridor rings. Just what I need. As I go to answer the phone, I quickly wipe my hands on my apron, but nobody is there. Now what? Ohh, the kitchen door is open! That's a bad omen. The milk carton on the counter is tipped over, and a white stream drips onto the floor. There crouches a guiltless Flori, licking the liquid dripping into his mouth.

under the chest, with the middle and index fingers between the front legs. The other hand simultaneously supports the rear. In this position a cat feels comfortable on your arm and held securely. It can also be carried this way.

Flori and Felix are occupied with Play 'n' Scratch, which is particularly entertaining for kittens; it is available in pet stores. The goal of this game is to catch the ball going around in the circle, or to play against one another. The cats can sharpen their claws on the scratch pad or catch the springy woolen tuft.

This Is My Territory

The kittens have grown bigger and increasingly independent. They are real personalities now and between **10 and 12 weeks of age,** have some more important rules of cat behavior to learn. An adventure playground in a secure yard provides the little ones with access to exciting natural stimuli.

independent...

ALTHOUGH THE KITTENS eat plenty several times a day, they still coax their mother into letting them nurse from time to time. And when Serafina and Isabella give in, the little ones clearly enjoy the physical closeness to their mothers, their tender grooming, and the familiar sucking. It doesn't seem to matter too much to the little ones that the milk is no longer flowing so abundantly.

Cat Training

Serafina and Isabella keep dragging morsels of food out of the bowl and into the hall, where they then call their children together by meowing loudly. Here's the pitch: "Here's your food. Eat up, for the milk bar is about to close." The mother cats spit and push away with their paws any persistent and imprudent youngsters that still want to suckle.

I almost pity the scolded kittens as they slink away, obviously hurt and confused, as if they don't understand that their childhood is coming to an end. But the mother cats know what they are doing, and foster an important weaning process to encourage their young ones to become more independent.

When Dad and Uncle Help Teach

Among other things, the unruly teens have also learned from the instruction of my two neutered

Flori is a teenager at the age of twelve weeks; five-year-old Jana, however, is still a little girl.

male cats, Dolittle and Lionel, that you don't simply pounce on and attack a grown cat and go unpunished. Now every kitten steps around them respectfully, and if the male cats allow it, cuddles up to them and gets a careful grooming. Dolittle especially loves his children, in particular his two daughters La Bomba and Sirena. They often lie down with Dad, arm in arm, on top of the scratching tree in the snoozing hollow, and they take midday siestas together. When one or both of the male cats feel like playing, they tumble and tussle all around the house with the young ones.

As they do so, the older cats carefully show their future male rivals who is boss in the house and territory. That's how the kittens learn to deal with other cats and grow up to be socially adjusted. Later on this will help them fit into an already existing feline social order. Anyone who takes a young kitten into a household with an established older cat is wise to be sure the new arrival has already learned all the important rules of conduct in its former residence.

The Dangers of Absolute Freedom

There is a busy street in front of our house. For their own protection, my cat family lives almost

Weeks 10 through 12

In my small, secure yard we have set up a nature/adventure playground for our indoor cats. Here La Bomba, Flori, and Sirena have discovered many new sensory stimuli: grass instead of carpet, fragrant, but prickly grain gleanings, and the air full of strange smells and sounds. That kind of outing in nature should take place only under supervision, though.

exclusively indoors. Much debate exists about whether this is an appropriate life for cats or a type of imprisonment. I personally have seen so many cats roaming around both in the country and in the city who have sooner or later paid for their freedom with their lives, that I recommend outings only under close supervision.

Many dangers threaten cats outdoors: thousands and thousands of cats are struck by cars, shot, and poisoned every year. Countless cats disappear, are stolen or are simply picked up by people because they are so pretty and trusting. Many die because they sneak into garages and cellars and get locked in accidentally. In addition, there can be problems with the neighbors, who may have little understanding and tolerance.

eeks 10 through 12

One animal friend is worried about a pet song-bird, and the other gets annoyed when a cat uses a carefully groomed flower bed for a litter box.

Many free-ranging cats have bitter fights with territorial rivals and return home every day with lots of bite wounds. Other cats like to jump through an open window into a neighbor's room to pay a little visit. You're lucky if that person is a cat lover. Otherwise the people won't be very enthusiastic if the cat takes a nap on their bed or leaves a hostess gift in the form of a mouse.

Our modern civilization is no longer a cat paradise. But as a cat owner, this is something you can provide for your cat at home. I have already described in part what an interesting, varied indoor cat environment should include.

Tip

To ensure good health, kittens are wormed for the second time at ten weeks; at eleven weeks, the shots are renewed (see page 56). Only then should they move to a new house.

67

How Cats Talk to Us

1

FRIENDLY GREETING: The cat comes over to you with tail held high, rubs against your legs, or rubs you with its head when you stroke it. The cat uses scent to mark its human, which means, "You belong to me."

2

FEELING FINE: The cat purrs and kneads with its paws on your lap. Its entire bearing is relaxed, and many cats close their eyes from sheer pleasure as they knead rhythmically.

3

SHOWING THE BELLY: Every cat instinctively tries to protect its tender underside from injuries, as in fights with other cats. If a cat turns its tummy to you, it is always a sign of great trust. It can be an invitation to play or to scratch the cat's tummy.

4

DEFENSE: The cat twitches its tail as it is petted. Perhaps you have touched the animal in a sensitive spot. Careful! Stop right away! If you misread the signal, there can be some painful consequences: raking the hand with the hind legs, a blow with the paw, or a bite.

5

LICKING: When you stroke your cat, it often gives you this sign of affection in return. When it licks your hand or your face, it's equivalent to "I like you, so I will pet you, too."

6

INSECURITY: The cat avoids eye contact with you, pulls back when you approach, and acts generally nervous. This behavior is often misinterpreted as a sign the cat feels offended. Try to figure out what you may have done to make the cat feel so insecure.

You will learn more about this in the following chapter, when the kittens move into their new homes.

Now let's go outdoors into the fresh air. I will describe for you how to set up a safe and pleasant playground in your yard.

An Adventure Playground in the Yard

Before you go outdoors with your cat, it should have the essential shots. The little ones know and trust their reference person and have learned to come when they're called. Practice this using the command, "Come!" plus the cat's name. Whenever the kitten is hungry, coax the animal and reward it with a treat that it really likes. In addition to vitamin paste and turkey ham, I use the little containers of treats. My cats recognize the sound, just as when I open a can of food. I shake it and call them, and they all come running. Okay, usually, if not always. A cat is always a cat, and sometimes it has more important things to do.

I have already explained why I think letting a cat run free without control and supervision is irresponsible and dangerous. But maybe you have a yard, or as I do, a small piece of property with a little shed, that you can make secure and interesting.

The size of the yard is not as important as the location and the type. The ideal is a quiet, little green area with lots of things to discover.

➤ Closely trimmed, empty grass surfaces are boring for cats. Let the wildflowers grow tall in part of your yard. Here the little predators can sneak around as if they were in a real wilderness

La Bomba is a natural-born photo model. She climbs the trellis like a pro and looks facetiously and saucily through the little window in the camera at precisely the right instant.

and exuberantly jump after butterflies and other insects or play hide-and-seek.

➤ For climbing, the best choices are fairly low deciduous trees with thick branches reaching out to the sides. Conifers are too prickly, and they quickly fill the fur with resin. Shrubs (with no thorns!) also provide hiding places.

Sylvester

HIGH SPIRITS ARE RARELY HELPFUL

The gang has been particularly wild today, romping all around the house. Whenever some other cat got in the way, it simply got run over. Sylvester even dared to pounce on my impressive, ten-year-old Maine Coon cat Lionel, who was taking his well-deserved midday siesta. He spun around lightning-quick, hissed loudly, and delivered a good swat with his paw. As well he should! Anyone who shows no respect for elders needs some remedial training. There must always be limits to patience. Sylvester learned his lesson quickly.

➤ Dripping and flowing water magically attracts all cats. This can be a spring, a calm pond with no fish, or a waterscape with a little stream and smooth stones. Gardening centers sell components that are ready to install.

➤ Fairly large pipes can be laid in a pile of leaves or twigs to tempt the kittens to crawl through them. Cats like all kinds of holes and hiding places.

➤ Even indoor cats love to climb, and like elevated perches. A fixed tree trunk with a board secured on top to lie on is ideal. Just be sure that the board doesn't hang over on one of the sides, so it's easier for the cat to climb onto it.

➤ Horizontal, raised wooden beams and tree trunks function like balance beams.

➤ Plant catnip and valerian, which put many cats into a trancelike state of happiness.

➤ At first the door to the house should always be kept open as a line of escape. Later the cats can learn how to use a cat door.

➤ Warning: No poisonous plants should be allowed to grow in the cat yard, since cats like to nibble on greens. Chemical toxins such as insecticides and weed killers must also be avoided!

Protective Fences

The best way to secure your yard or a part of it is with an electric fence for small animals. This consists of dark green nylon netting with thin metal wires that carry the current. A fence charger is the source of the current, and it is plugged into a wall socket or a 6-volt battery. It must not be a closed electrical circuit. To allay your fears, these special small animal fences, available from

pet shops, are absolutely harmless, and mustn't be confused with the common electric fences for large animals that are ten times stronger. The main thing is to be sure that the fence is installed properly before the first time the cats are let out.

Here's how it works: if a cat tries to slip through the mesh (about 2¾ inches [7 cm]), it gets a brief, unpleasant, but entirely harmless shock. The effect is amazing, for the kittens quickly learn to respect this barrier. Many of my cat friends and I have used this type of fence for years with great success

Thanks to their now fully developed physical abilities and an outstanding sense of balance, La Bomba and Sirena can balance securely on the beam. They can even turn around without falling off.

Photos from left to right:
With tail held high in greeting, Felix trots over to his human.
Now the pace is a cat gallop!
A strange dog in my territory? Flori tries to look dominant. However, his tucked-in tail shows that he is afraid.
Felix, too, puffs himself up and arches his back. He is sending clear threat signals and stares at his antagonist. The other should take care to keep a safe distance away.

and with no bad experiences, as long as it was properly installed from the outset. A further advantage is that the fence keeps out intruders such as strange cats and wild animals.

Cindy Comes for a Visit

My friend has a nice, little, female Poodle that has been accustomed to cats and loved them ever since she was little. So Cindy is welcome to accompany her mistress to the cookout in my yard today. I want to photograph the kittens' behavior and introduce them to a dog. Cindy has learned that she mustn't chase cats and to check first to see who is interested in playing with her.

First we let the dog into the secure yard so that it can get familiar with the strange cat scents. In the meantime, La Bomba, Felix, and Flori are inside the shed. Then they change places so that the dog and the cats, all of which have a good sense of smell, have plenty of time and opportunity to inspect one another's usual trail. Next, my friend takes Cindy for a long walk so that the dog gets a chance to burn off some energy. That is important, for even though Cindy is nice and well trained, she is also very lively. And for the first encounter, it's a good idea for Cindy to be calm and relaxed. That's the way she remains, and she cautiously goes up to the cats. She wags her tail in a friendly way. This dog body language is

Tip

If you want to learn cat language, pay attention to body language, the position of the ears and tail, the expression in the eyes, the body's posture, and vocalizations. Cat talk is really not so difficult.

equivalent to, "Hi there. Let's be friends." But the cat sees the dog as a monster with a tail flipping back and forth, which it interprets in cat language as meaning, "Watch out! High tension!" So at first the cat tries to assert its ownership of its territory: trying to play the hero, it arches its back, stands its hair on end, and stares at the antagonist. The pupils open wide with excitement. Flori shows the most fear and tucks in his tail. La Bomba acts like a stiff-legged bottlebrush, and

Felix howls like a warrior before an attack. Cindy evidently is impressed by the heroic displays, for she turns around and lies down at our feet. After a while the cats slink gradually closer, for their curiosity gets the better of them, and they sniff around to see what kind of strange creature is lying there. And finally they follow one another on an inspection tour of the yard. Cindy follows La Bomba, and Felix is behind Cindy. Flori crouches above in the apple tree and is content to

Careful, little La Bomba! If you had surprised a bee on the sunflower, you would have learned a painful lesson, and would have a swollen paw.

watch the whole thing from a safe height. Suppose he knows that dogs can't climb?

It takes just a few hours for Cindy, Felix, and La Bomba to be romping around together in the yard. We owe it to the good Poodle that this has gone so quickly and smoothly, for she is an experienced "cat dog." Naturally, Cindy gets a sausage and every cat gets a piece of chicken breast as a treat. Finally even Flori comes down from the tree, and they all tear around through the tall wildflowers that I have let grow in one corner. But this is an unfair game, for the cats keep disappearing up the trees and Cindy has to stay down below. That can irritate even a very good dog, and Cindy barks loudly. But it was an exciting experience for all of us. Doesn't Felix look impressive in the photo on the right on page 73?

Faithful Dog, False Cat?

"House cats are like many other felines: born loners. In contrast to dogs, which are pack animals, they have never learned to get along and live with their own kind. They are independent, self-centered, unfaithful creatures, and you never know where you stand with them." Is this opinion just a prejudice, a half truth, or is there some truth to it?

It's true that most, but not all, wild cats live a solitary existence. Wolves, on the other hand, the wild ancestors and originators of today's dogs, live and hunt in packs. It is also true, to the

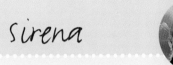

Sirena

SIRENA PROVIDES TOTAL WELLNESS

When everything is quiet in the house, I, too, enjoy the calm. Often I retreat to my bedroom and meditate or listen with eyes closed—as I do this evening—to music for meditation. At one point I feel something soft and warm touching me. Sirena has tiptoed in to be with me. She rolls happily on my lap and begins to purr. And as the murmur of distant ocean waves emanates from the CD, Sirena purrs like a quiet motor whose gentle vibration resonates on my abdominal walls. I spontaneously give off sounds in harmony with Sirena's purring and sink into a wonderful, deep state of relaxation. What a gift to have a cat for a friend. It helps us people to get rid of stress and recharge our batteries. A cat is the best wellness program I know of.

What's this umbrella for? To keep off the sun?
It's really not that hot.

Top photo: Flori seems to be smirking. Suppose
he suspects something?

Middle and bottom photos: La Bomba performs
a little interlude. My, what is that? A spray of water
tumbling down from above? Get down quick, close
the eyes and stick out the claws! La Bomba didn't
get wet, but she doesn't like that kind of joke. Watch
out, photographer, if I ever get a hold of you! Don't
you know that cats can't stand water?

As the kittens develop their personalities, they form true friendships with one another.

extent that this comparison is fair, that a dog strives in its heart of hearts to be accepted by its pack and live among it. That's why a healthy pack structure with respect to its human is so immensely important to it.

Cats don't have this dependence, but they form voluntary associations with their humans and other cats. These still can be friendly and loving relationships. Cats are perceived as independent, fickle, and self-centered only because they come and go as they please. And if that's impossible, they react with outlandish behavior. So far no one has succeeded in completely deciphering the mysteries of the cat. And that's fine, because that's why we love them.

Cat Friendships and Peacemakers

In my cat community, the Maine Coon Lionel is the peacemaker. He's the cat in the group that steps in when two cats fight or when an animal behaves too aggressively with the community. Often all he has to do is appear in front of the antagonists and look at them. At other times he jumps fiercely into the conflict and separates the combatants with a couple of blows from his paws. Then peace reigns again.

Quarrels even occur among sociable indoor cats that live together, but generally they are harmless. Depending on their feelings toward one another, most of the time my cats sleep together, groom each other, and play together.

In the course of developing their personalities, the kittens have formed clearly recognizable friendships. I plan on preserving these in the near future when I give them away. Sensitive Frederick is especially fond of his pretty sister Bonita, and cheerful Felix, who always has something to tell, likes fluffy little Pauli. And Papa Dolittle prefers to cuddle with his daughters Sirena and La Bomba. Lively La Bomba, who in the meantime, is working on a film, will remain with us with our cover kitten and offspring, Sylvester and Flori.

What Is a Dream Kitten?

Maybe you know the fairy tale about the frog king or the ugly duckling. I know stories about poor, half-starved, disheveled kittens that have been taken in by people and through loving care have turned into beautiful dream cats. Some people also find their dream partner or dream job totally by chance.

I love those kinds of fairy tales and stories, I trust my experience in real life, and try to make such dreams come true by taking my own specific steps. I have learned it's possible to avoid many, if not all, disappointments in advance.

The term *dream kitten* probably means something different to every person. But through decades of experience in finding homes for cats, I have summarized a few of the desires that all my applicants and future owners have expressed:

What ideas these humans come up with! They hollow out a pumpkin, carve a gruesome face on it, and light it up with a candle to scare people. They call this celebration Halloween. Twelve-week-old Frederick is amazed. Suppose he thinks the red-glowing pumpkin face is a cat's head? No matter. The main thing is that there's some tasty tuna fish behind it.

➤ A dream kitten is people-oriented and affectionate. It likes to be with its family, and it develops into a family member that's respected and beloved by all.

➤ It has a stable, well-balanced nature, with no traumatic baggage from its early days. The kitten is thus in a position to face new situations with self-reliance and knows how to assert itself.

➤ This type of kitten is never boring, and is no listless couch tiger. It likes to play, is alert, and is full of surprises. The animal is attentive and active, without being obtrusive. This balance must, of course, be returned by the human.

➤ The dream kitten is healthy and has no chronic illnesses or genetic problems. Nobody can guarantee this with 100 percent certainty, but it's important to do everything possible to be sure. Of course the little one has to be wormed, vaccinated, and come from a cat family in which health care is maintained.

➤ Like all dreams, the dream creature is beautiful so that the person falls in love with it right away. It doesn't matter if it has long or short hair, or is of slight or powerful build. Many people automatically fall for little bears with little pug noses, whereas others fall for elegant gazelles with green, almond-shaped eyes. And even an unprepossessing gray mouse can win over a heart spontaneously, as long as it has that special something that we call *charisma* in people. If mutual love exists, between a person and an animal, that love needs to be maintained.

Test:
Which Kitten Is Right for Me?

Yes No

1. You want a clean indoor cat, and the little ones you are interested in have been raised that way.

2. When you visit them, the kittens run over to you curiously and let you pet them.

3. The kittens are fully wormed and have had all their shots.

4. The kitten is at least twelve weeks old when offered for adoption.

5. You asked plenty of questions of the owner/breeder and got good answers.

6. The owner/breeder will personally bring the kittens to their new homes.

7. The living conditions impress you as clean. You are able to look at and get to know all the cats living there.

If you can answer all the questions with a definite yes, you have found one or two dream kittens in a good home. If not, you need to keep searching.

Heading Out into the New World

The kittens are bubbling over with liveliness and unbridled energy. They want to conquer new territories. **By the thirteenth week** the little tigers have learned all the important things. Now it's my duty to be sure that they go to nice people and feel totally comfortable in their new homes.

The New Home...

DOES THIS HAPPEN TO YOU, TOO? Sometimes it appears as though the minutes and seconds creep by slowly and other times it seems that weeks and months just fly by like seconds, so that one wishes they could be brought to a standstill. Whenever this is the case, we are usually having a slice of life full of joy, happiness, and activity. That's how the last three months have been as we've shared them with our kittens and the four adults: a stimulating, intensive time during which we had many good laughs over the comical adventures of the little rogues.

Time to Say Good-Bye

But now I think even my fairly spacious house with a large attic for playing and romping has become too small for eleven whirlwinds. And even with all the attention we have devoted to them, no one can treat so many cats properly over the long haul.

Even Isabella and Serafina, both of whom were devoted mothers, now need a longer break to catch their breath, build up their strength, and tend to their own needs. It's time for all of us to part and say "good-bye" and accept that it's best for the kittens, even though it's particularly difficult for me this time. For their further development, the kittens need their own territories and

Jana likes to use a wand with feathers when playing with Pipo; that way, a paw swipe strikes the "prey" and not her hand.

Weeks 13 through 15

people who can devote time and attention to them.

I have no doubts that I will find the perfect places for our dream kittens. But before I tell you about choosing the right partners and giving the kittens up for adoption, first save all the advice and recommendations that I give to each of my new cat owners along the way. They, along with the other tips you have read, are based on twenty years of personal experience.

Even though my intentions were always good, I admit that at the beginning I too made mistakes. You can learn from these experiences and provide a proper home for your cats right from the outset. If your love for the animal makes that possible, no kitten will want to live anywhere but with you.

People and Their Homes

I have often visited couples with children at their homes where I've immediately had the feeling that only adults lived there. It's hard to imagine that no overexcited little creature has bounced around on the white couch, or left toys lying around in the living room. The beige carpeting looks spotless and untouched, as if it has been walked on only by children's feet in perpetually clean socks. And there are never any traces of a child visible anywhere. I pity the child who is

forced to live in such a sterile, cold environment. These people really want a kitten. But these are not the right surroundings for either a child or a kitten.

Of course, there is also the precise opposite of the home just described: tiny rooms crammed so full of furniture and meaningless knickknacks that you can hardly turn around in them. Before I pay a visit here, I prefer to stop en route to use a restroom rather than the one in the house, because everything is so messy and dirty.

Anyone who has worked in the animal protection field is familiar with plenty of such chaotic homes. Often there are completely neglected animals, which ostensibly were taken in through an exaggerated love of animals. Thirty and more cats in a two-room apartment are not uncommon.

This photo was possible only because the calm Flori had not yet been bitten by hunting fever when these two mice boldly and unsuspectingly walked the tightrope in front of his nose.

The Way Cats Want to Live

Many people prefer to have a cat rather than a dog, because they think that cats are less demanding. But this is only partly true. In fact, you don't have to take kitty for a walk several times a day. And it is better at being left alone, although not too much; it doesn't bark, and it's smaller than most dogs. However, cats need adequate space in the home territory to burn off their excess, stored-up energy. They also need varied, stimulating play, adequate attention, and an arrangement that meets their requirements as closely as possible.

A Tree for Climbing and Scratching

If you are among the clever hobbyists who can construct an area for climbing and scratching, you will make your cats happy. But if you, like I, are not good at making things and have too little time to do it yourself, your only choice is to purchase a cat tree. Here are some important things to consider as you do:

As the designation *scratching and climbing tree* indicates, this item should fulfill two functions for the cat: it should serve to sharpen the claws, and it should function as climbing and gymnastics equipment. Here's the basic rule: the tree has to be stable, and must not wobble or tip over easily. And quality comes with a price!

Lean toward the high-quality products from pet supply stores, rather than unsuitable climb-

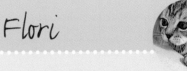

Flori

MOUSE TELEVISION

Among all the kittens Flori is the most good-natured. He loves to play and tumble, but he's never as wild as the others. His favorite thing is to sit by the open screened window and watch the birds outside and the people passing by. So one day I get the idea to let him watch a little television. Since he's not interested in thrillers, I put a large mouse cage on the floor; the bars are spaced closely enough that no cat paw can reach through. Flori looks on with interest as the lively mice named Fleck, Speck, and Dreck scramble out of their pile of leaves and roots and go over to their food dish. Flori presses his nose right up to the mesh. Fleck comes over and gives it a bite. Frightened and bewildered, Flori pulls his head back. Yes, even a tiny mouse is capable of defending its territory. Flori hadn't figured on that.

Isabella and her fourteen-week-old kitten Felix enjoy eating cypress grass. You can also offer your indoor cats blades of grass and greens from indoor bamboo and grains to help them regurgitate the hairballs that form in their stomachs when they groom themselves. No poisonous plants belong in a house with cats, though. If present, they must be removed.

ing trees that tempt inexperienced cat owners mainly through their low price. Steer away from this worthless trash! Usually the cat uses such things once and never again. A short while ago as I was visiting someone and leaned on the perch of such a cheap new acquisition, the perch broke right off. Other climbing trees are unstable and wobbly. In such cases, kitty much prefers to shred your expensive armchair, and that's precisely what you are trying to prevent.

Further nonsense is a cat-condo attached to the bottom of the scratching post, supposedly to make these climbing trees better suited to cats. Whoever consulted with the cats about this? In the first place, all couch tigers prefer high places with a good view. Secondly, these cumbersome boxes interfere with access to the scratching tree, where the cat prefers to sharpen its claws.

Here's what the ideal climbing and scratching tree looks like:

➤ It's as tall as the room so that it can be secured to the floor and the ceiling.

➤ The first 3 feet (80 cm) or so of the trunk wrapped in sisal rope are accessible so that the cat can stretch upward without interference and sharpen its claws with pleasure. Only thereafter should there be condos, perches, and nooks for sleeping.

➤ Instead of sisal trunks, wood can be used. The little tigers prefer the soft woods of poplar, linden, and fig.

➤ The sleeping nooks are rectangular wood or metal frames lined with plush that are securely bolted to the trunk. Cats love these sleeping trays because the fabric conforms to their body. You will quickly note that all the cats prefer to lie in

Test:
Is Your Home Comfortable for Cats?

Yes	No	
○	○	1. Does your home have at least two rooms plus a kitchen and a bath, and does the cat have free access to all rooms?
○	○	2. Are there screens on all open windows and on the balcony, if present?
○	○	3. Is there a stable climbing tree for scratching, plus one or two cat shelves?
○	○	4. Does the cat always have a clean litter box to use and is there one litter box per cat?
○	○	5. Are there food dishes and two separate water bowls? Is there a small indoor fountain with cypress grass?
○	○	6. Are there comfortable sitting places on cabinets, bookcases, and windowsills and a climbing tree as tall as the room?
○	○	7. Do boxes, cat condos, baskets, cat beds, and corners offer hiding places and resting spots?

Could you answer all the questions with a yes? A gold medal for you. If not, I recommend supplying the missing items for the benefit of your cat.

Exercise and daily play are fun and keep small and large tigers in good condition.

high places, and that they often compete with one another for the spot with the best view.

➤ Make sure that the trunks can be re-covered with sisal, and that the plush fabric can be replaced when it gets scratched through. Otherwise you'll have to replace the whole scratching tree with a new one.

➤ Don't set up the scratching apparatus in just any corner where it's out of the way or in some spot in the house you happen to have free.

This important piece of equipment belongs where the family likes to be. That means within sight of the armchair, preferably with a view out the window, and ideally, onto all passageways. It's in a cat's nature to watch from an elevated position and see who is coming into the territory for a visit, and to miss nothing when something interesting is going on.

Where's the Toilet, Please?

I know a few indoor cats that follow their owners into the toilet, because that's where their litter box is, and they use it at the same time their humans are there. Others prefer concealed places set aside for their use alone. My six large litter boxes are divided between two floors. When visitors are coming, and the litter boxes have just been freshened up, one of my tigers will always walk immediately to the box in the entryway. Then it scratches around importantly and as noisily as possible inside, leaves a fragrant souvenir, and proudly marches off with head held high. The cat doesn't care about the "air quality." Two-leggeds need to know who's at home here in the territory.

➤ Whether your cat prefers an open litter box or one with a cover usually depends on what it got used to in the place where it spent the first months of its life. I prefer litter boxes with a cover, because my cats scratch around so wildly in the litter that otherwise everything would come flying out. I don't use or recommend covers with a flap on the front, for that produces a buildup of ammonia fumes from the combina-

Time for play. An excited fourteen-week-old Flori tries to catch the tuft of feathers with a bell hanging on the end of a cat pole. That's not so easy with his little belly. La Bomba, who is more slender, can jump a little higher.

Soon they will have to part, for at the age of thirteen weeks they are old enough to go their own ways. But the littermates can have one more adventure outing together. And as you can see, they are happiest when they can stay close together on their discoveries for now.

Top photo: Sirena, Flori, and Pipo look alert. Was there something moving in the grass over there?

Middle photo: Sirena and Flori climb around on the little birch as deftly as adults.

Bottom photo: Whoops! Sirena and Pipo have lost their balance on the small branch. Still, they don't fall down, but instead hang on as skillfully as acrobats.

Soon the kittens will have to be separated, for at the age of thirteen weeks they are old enough to go their own ways.

tion of urine and heat. And kitty doesn't like miniature litter boxes designed to save space. A litter box should be large enough for the cat to turn around inside.

➤ One litter box per cat, please! If you have two cats, you need two litter boxes, and in different places, for many cats are very territorial with regard to their litter box. This can even lead to fighting. Or one cat may refuse to use the litter box because the other has already been there.

➤ The right place is important. You can put one litter box in the bathroom, but not near the shower. A dreaded spray of water might frighten the cat. The other one should be in a quiet spot in the house. Never place the boxes near the food dishes or the scratching tree. Like humans, cats don't like to go to the toilet where they eat or sleep.

➤ The litter must be absorbent and have a natural feel. Scented additives appeal to our noses, but cats seldom like them. Clumping litter made from bentonite swells and forms hard clumps when it encounters fluid, so urine can be scooped out when solid waste is removed. In spite of its higher cost, it's cheaper in the long run because you use less of it. The litter should be kept about 3 inches (7 cm) deep in the litter box.

➤ Cleanliness is the main thing. All cats are very sensitive to smell, and many problems with uncleanliness come from neglected litter boxes. It's better to clean too much rather than too little, and when it's time to clean the litter box completely to scrub out the litter box thoroughly with hot water and dry it.

I'm Hiding! Come Find Me!

A bleak apartment with no hiding places is not only boring, but for a cat it's also about as appealing as a café in a parking garage. You don't always have to have expensive baskets and condos for hiding places. You can also use sturdy boxes with a lining or washable sheepskin. The "caves" are best divided among corners or on cupboards and bookcases. Cats also love hanging sofa slipcovers and bedspreads for crawling under. But be careful! One day my little ones discovered a hiding place between the springs of an old armchair. If a heavy person had sat on it, that could have resulted in a bad situation. All kinds of dresser drawers, open cupboard doors, and hiding places behind sofa cushions are in especially high demand, as well as washing machines and dryers, since they smell of humans. Keep them closed, and before you turn on the machines, look inside!

The Perfect Place for Every Cat

People who care that their kittens have the best living conditions and go to loving people should pay attention to the following:

➤ If you don't have advance orders for your kittens among close acquaintances, it's a good idea to place simultaneous notices in two or three newspapers. That gives you the greatest selection of applicants. I always formulate my announcements a bit cleverly and clearly describe the advantages as follows: raised in a family, affectionate, good indoor cat, and so forth.

➤ Never lose patience if things don't click right away. Sometimes I have found great places even

La Bomba

A KITTEN WENT FLYING BY . . .

La Bomba has never seen blue, shimmering dragonflies. With twitching tail, she lies in ambush in the grass and watches them whirr past her. Then suddenly a leap, a swipe with the paw, and splash! La Bomba catches the dragonfly, but in her enthusiasm for the hunt, she forgot that there is a pond behind the reeds. That's not the end of the world, for swimming is really no problem for kittens. Still, as I dry the sopping La Bomba with a towel, she doesn't seem to find things as comical as I do. A refreshing bath just isn't something a kitten appreciates.

for older cats. You sometimes have to wait until the right person comes along.

➤ There are times when you shouldn't give away a kitten for reasons of animal welfare. From May to October there are countless animal shelter cats and barnyard cats looking for homes. And no cat wants to be left alone during vacation right after its adoption.

➤ Don't give cats away for free. This attracts people who place no value on the animal, and then at the first opportunity may turn the animal away. If you are interested in receiving a kitten, remember that in most cases free cats have not had their shots when they are given away. Anyone who takes in that kind of animal may have to deal with illness caused by the stress of moving and the attendant immune system weakness.

➤ Animal shelters usually collect a fee when they place an animal for adoption. Purebred cats with papers may be priced at $400 to $650 or more, depending on the breed and market value. I personally charge for the cost of shots, plus a small additional sum of money. I use these funds to help support the cat section of a St. Francis of Assisi animal shelter (see page 119). That's how I get the money to support orphaned cats.

➤ Before I invite people over who are interested in my cats, I speak with them in detail by phone. It's my experience that good prospective owners are happy to answer my questions. And of course they can ask questions of me. I soon say good-bye to people who prefer to remain anonymous, as if they were buying a couple of rolls in a supermarket.

➤ In addition, each of my new owners must sign an adoption contract that contains protective

provisions for the kitten. Such contracts make sense only if they are checked out by a lawyer. After one painful experience a few years ago, I now use the adoption contract used by animal shelters.

➤ There are two advantages to your personally delivering the kitten to its new home: you can get another look at the new home, and the kittens don't feel like they've been simply evicted, since they are introduced to their new home by a trusted person. That makes their new start a little easier.

La Bomba looks at the little pond with fascination. She is a careful kitten who knows exactly how one gets their feet wet. She throws all caution to the wind only when she's excited by the chase (see the story on page 92).

The Arrival of the Applicants

Anyone who wants to get a cat for his family from me has to come for a visit with the whole family. For if there's one person in the group who doesn't like the animal, the cat will sense it sooner or later. I set aside an hour or more for the people I have invited over. I let the children play with the kitten, watch the parents, and see how they all behave around the animals.

It's always exciting for me to see who chooses whom. Sometimes it's love at first sight; at other times the decision goes back and forth. And it can also happen that a person absolutely wants a particular cat, but the chosen cat tries to avoid the person. Even though I may see nothing negative in the petitioner's behavior during the visit, I trust and respect the cat's decision.

Lively, alert La Bomba is the one that's always ahead by a nose on outdoor expeditions, even if it's only to sniff the blossoms on the heather.

Happiness in Pairs

Often people call me who are desperate to find a kitten as company for the single, bored indoor cat they already have. As long as the older cat is still playful and youthful, you have no choice but to support the decision. But a pair of cats can also produce lots of stress for all the four- and two-legged creatures living there.

For example, if you put a ten-year-old cat together with a three-month-old youngster, it's like forcing a seventy-year-old person and a schoolchild to spend all their time living together. How do you think that would work? The old cat, with its greater need for peace and calm, will eventually become irritated by the countless invitations to play from the exuberant kitten. And the kitten will have to pursue its own needs all by itself. In this case a well-socialized cat of a similar age would be better company for the older cat.

Also, for reasons of disposition and development, some cats prove to be better off as loners, and they don't want to share their territory and person with other cats.

People who want to keep their cat exclusively in a house or apartment should get two cats right at the outset. The best candidates for living together are two littermates, or cats that have grown up together and have already formed friendships. Because my dream kittens were permitted to select their new homes and owners, this time I was able to place them all by pairs in their new homes. Only La Bomba, Sylvester, and Flori stayed with us.

Sylvester

A BIRTHDAY WITH A FIREMAN

The birthday cake is on the table—a beauty, with plenty of decoration and five candles to symbolize each decade of life. After the candles are blown out and the cake is cut, one of my guests gets the idea of lighting the candles again because it looks so nice. Why not? The cats are outside in the hall. But someone leaves the door open. All at once Sylvester is there, and with a single bound jumps onto the chair and the table. Very elegant, as always—you have to give him that. He landed precisely, without knocking anything over. But what about his bushy tail in my guests' faces? In spite of my love of cats, I can't excuse that, Sylvester. Yuck, something is burning, and it smells horrible! Even before I grasp what is going on, a guest has the presence of mind to extinguish Sylvester's tail in a large glass of cold punch. It's good to have a fireman as a guest.

New Friendships for Life

Eight kittens have now left me and successfully taken charge of their new territories. And the hearts of their people, too, from the look of things. They are all happy with their new four-legged family members. What stimulating and fun things the cats experience after their **fourth month of life**, I will tell you in this last chapter.

New Found Happiness...

FELIX AND PAULI, two of Isabella's kids, were not selected as superstars for this book. However, the happiness that they brought to their human family is so special that I want to tell you about it.

When the family introduced themselves to me, I was at first skeptical. They were looking for a cat for their sight-disabled two-year-old son Max, who had been born prematurely. The family had heard that animals are good for children with disabilities and can help them along. Because of his visual impairment, Max can only distinguish between dark and light, and has thus fallen behind in his other development. Because the parents were nice on the phone, I decided to chance it, and I invited them all over, including their fourteen-year-old daughter.

I will never forget the way they all sat together in my kitchen. Little Max crouched on the floor, flailed about with his arms, and said something that only his mother understood. For me his speech sounded totally unintelligible. Almost all the grown-up and young cats were playing with the parents and the elder daughter Jessica, shunning Max. Evidently Max's utterings and uncontrolled movements made my cats uneasy. But Felix didn't let that bother him, and neither did his previously cautious sister Pauli.

Felix licks the tip of Alexandra's nose. This loving gesture says, "I like you." In the meantime Pascha has comfortably fallen asleep.

Months 4 through 6

The two of them sat in front of the child, even though the youngster didn't try to touch them, and I had the feeling that the kittens had made their choice. The mother especially won me over by carefully encouraging her son to behave gently with the kittens. A week later their house was set up properly for the cats, following my advice and I personally delivered the two littermates.

Felix the Child Therapist

I know that dolphins and dogs are helpful to children with disabilities. But what about a headstrong cat? Was it a good omen that I baptized the little cat Felix? (In Latin, Felix means "the happy one.") Like all my kittens, Felix is very affectionate and especially fond of humans. But based on his character, I would describe him rather as a mixture of turbulent hoodlum and prattler. He's always muttering about something. This is a trait that he inherited from his father, Dolittle, for his British Shorthair mother is quite a silent cat, except when she has babies.

And Felix, the happy one, accomplished something that no one had ever expected of him. For weeks he lay with the little boy in bed, talked to him, and licked his tummy. Max touched the cat for the first time after six weeks. And one day he freely followed the cat down the hall to the living room. The mother said this was a small miracle, something the physical therapist who regularly works with him hadn't managed to accomplish in six months. In the meantime, Max can distinguish which of the two cats comes over to him, even though he can't see them clearly. By the way, Felix and Pauli share the child care duties.

When the therapist who works with Max because of his severe visual impairment comes into the house, Felix regularly absents himself and lies in his snoozing spot on top of the

Sirena

FLYING GLOW LAMPS

There is one game that my kittens particularly enjoy: chasing after points of light, such as sunbeams, which I capture with the help of a small mirror and play over the floor and walls. Then Sirena and Dolittle discover something unique at their new home in the month of June: flying dots of light that come in through the open terrace door. Catching them is great fun, for the light always goes out as soon as Sirena touches it with her paw. Poor little glowworms, how could they know that Sirena merely wants to play with them?

scratching tree. Pauli, on the other hand, sits with Max and his therapist and watches the whole training program with interest.

Dolittle and Sirena

The father and daughter moved together into a beautiful house with a nice family with two children, aged ten and twelve. In the spring, Mr. E. was already remodeling his terrace into a sort of enclosure with a gate to the yard. The cats aren't the only ones who spend their free time there. Sometimes they also use a leash and a breast harness to go out into the little yard, for the grass there tastes better than the grass grown in the house.

Dolittle always wants his breakfast punctually in the morning. That has continued with his new family. If the people ever seem inclined not to get up, he makes sure they get out of bed quickly. Either Dolittle licks their faces with his rough tongue, or he tenderly but unmistakably nibbles a toe sticking out from under the blankets. It didn't take long for the two cats to train their family. At first they lived mostly upstairs in the two children's rooms, but now they rule the whole house. And in the evening, when the cats are playing with the cat pole with its multicolored tuft of feathers, it may happen that the 13 pound (6 kg) cat forgets himself in the battle with the prey and pounces onto the father resting on the couch. But no one in this family objects to that. Sometimes the rooster comes for a visit from the neighbor's yard with his harem of hens.

The same ritual is repeated every morning: Mrs. E. opens the screened windows to let in the

air, and both cats jump onto the windowsill to look out. Then the rooster marches under the window, sees the two predators on the windowsill above, and calls out with such a bloodcurdling cry that both cats immediately bound away.

But woe betide our neighbor's cat if it dares to step into the territory. Then it's Dolittle's move. He puffs himself up to twice his size, stares at the intruder, and hisses so frightfully through the screen that the other cat immediately takes to its heels.

The red cat Dolittle puts his arm around his seven-month-old daughter Sirena, who cuddles comfortably and happily with her father. I didn't want to split up this love, so the two of them went to their new home together.

The cover cat Sylvester, now at the age of seventeen weeks, meets up with my rabbit Hannibal.

Hannibal lays his ears back and sniffs the cat, which still looks calmly at the camera.

"Let me take a sniff. Who is this?"

Sylvester spits. "That doesn't mean I'm afraid of him." Hannibal grooms himself calmly. "It's not so bad." Hannibal lies down on the floor to cuddle, and Sylvester grooms the rabbit. A friendship is born.

Other than that, all two- and four-leggeds are very happy together. Many things stay the same. Dolittle purrs as high as a chirping bird when he's petted, and before he takes a drink from his bowl, he touches the water with his paw. Aside from cuddling, eating is Dolittle's favorite pastime, and the family has to make sure he doesn't gobble up Sirena's portion as well as his own. Sirena is just the same as she was when she was a kitten: a captivating, gentle princess who knows how to bewitch everyone who gets to know her.

Frederick and Bonita

Frederick and his sister Bonita live with a childless couple who both work as physical therapists. Since their practice is located in their house, the

cats are never left alone for long. The two litter-mates don't appear to be bored in the roomy house. They know how to keep themselves busy.

When they are not tearing through the house or climbing on the scratching tree, Bonita and Frederick crouch together in one of the net-covered windows and spend hours watching the goings-on outdoors. And as Mrs. S. told me on the phone, not even a storm with a downpour, thunder, and lightning can drive them from their spot, which is quite uncommon for cats.

The liking for water that Bonita has developed over time is also uncommon. When her humans are taking a bath or a shower, Bonita is always there. As soon as you have finished and turned off the water, she jumps into the tub and rolls around happily in the remaining puddles of water.

Tip

If cats and small house pets such as rabbits or guinea pigs share the same space, be sure the cats can never hunt or bite the prey. Any meeting should take place only under close supervision.

Favorite Cat Games

1 BALL GAMES: Everything that rolls, bounces, or can be pursued and caught is extremely interesting. Whether a ping-pong ball, a wad of paper, a cork, or a rubber ball, cats are really gifted ball handlers. They dribble, dive in the air, and play goalie, and many of them will even retrieve.

2 FUNLIGHT: A ray of sun reflected on a pocket mirror, or a small point of light from a flashlight blinks and flits through the room. Even jaded indoor tigers come to life and turn into wild light hunters.

3 HIDING: Cats love doing this best under the sofa or bed, or behind a tablecloth. Their tails flick excitedly on the floor, their bottoms wave back and forth. Then all of a sudden there's a pounce, and back they go into concealment—priceless.

4 SNACK BALL: You can buy these plastic balls filled with treats in pet supply stores. The cat's task is to roll the ball around until a treat rolls out. The size of the hole, and thus the degree of difficulty, is controlled by a small slide.

5 PAWING: Forepaws are to cats what our hands are to us. Wiggle a toy mouse on a string back and forth inside a box with holes. Your cat will paw around, as in a mouse hole, and play enthusiastically.

6 BED GAME: Before I get up in the morning, I scratch with my finger under the blankets until my cat makes a pounce for the prey and sometimes bites down (that's part of the deal). But don't worry: the blanket acts as protection. I advise against wiggling bare toes out from under the bedclothes.

Right after their arrival, both cats started scooping the potting soil out of the flowerpots. A stern "No!" had no effect, so I advised the owners to squirt them with a stream of water from the plant mister. This gentle training measure almost always works. It has the advantage that the cat doesn't connect the punishment directly with its human, so there is no loss of trust. But at that time I didn't know anything about Bonita's love of water. Whereas Frederick left the flowerpots alone after getting sprayed a second time, Bonita really enjoyed the little shower. A loud clap with the hands worked with her.

One day Mrs. S. was replacing her curtains in the bedroom. She chose a diaphanous material with colorful printed butterflies. Frederick and Bonita were uncontainable. They went hunting for the pretty butterflies. Mrs. S. had no choice but to exchange the curtains and buy a new toy: a small, colorful butterfly made of soft material on a string. Now the cats can play "catch the butterfly" as well as "catch the mouse." At the age of eight months, Bonita came into heat, and Frederick had to be kept in a separate room. But while he waited behind closed doors, there was a different black cat on the wall near the screened window. And as Bonita meowed loudly and stuck her behind through the screen . . . No, contrary to what you're thinking, nothing happened. It was another female cat, and it lost interest in Bonita's desire. A short time after Bonita came into heat, the two cats were neutered. It's risky to spay a cat while she's in heat. According to the newest medical discoveries, ideally a cat should be spayed or neutered between the ages of five and six months.

At four months Flori has already become a large, powerful cat. And if something rustles in the autumn leaves, he excitedly crouches down, just as a cat should.

And the Others...

Two of Serafina's kittens, Amadeus and Pascha, immediately won the heart of ten-year-old Melanie, and they have since lived with mother and daughter in a first-floor apartment with a small yard. Pascha, who always went his own way and did only what he wanted when he was young, is very sociable in his new home. Amadeus, still a supreme cuddler, greets all visitors and wants them to pet him. Melanie is a conscientious cat friend who explains to all her friends precisely how to behave with the animals.

Isabella's son Pipo lives with one-year-old Kara, likewise one of my cats, in a comfortable apartment with a large, secured balcony. The spayed Kara at first mothered little Pipo too much. Pipo thus became so rebellious in adolescence that the female cat had a hard time getting any respect from him. His behavior improved only after he was neutered, and now the two of them get along fine together.

Daily cuddling sessions with their people are important for cats and a pleasure for both. When you pet two cats simultaneously, you avoid creating jealousy. Otherwise, you have to be careful to avoid shortchanging one of them. The photo shows Frederick and Pascha at four months.

Pay Attention to Temperament

In my experience female cats usually prefer to live with polite, gentle male cats such as Flori. The rough play and macho swaggering of many male cats often poses problems for sensitive female cats.

Therefore, it is important for all cats living together to have compatible temperaments. For example, you should never place an exceptionally shy and insecure cat with a very decisive, domineering one. Otherwise, it could happen that the weaker one may be oppressed and end up developing behavioral problems.

In my cat group, the peacemaker Lionel maintains peace and order. Even Serafina, a type of female cat-in-chief, has to keep her dominance under control; otherwise, Lionel will rein her in. The order of precedence is not as clearly established in a cat community as it is in a dog pack. It can change, and when a female cat has young ones, she automatically rises to prominence and is treated with more respect by the others.

At My House ...

It has become more quiet in the house. The older cats, especially the two mothers, enjoy the time they now have for themselves. Only the three

Frederick

THE DISAPPEARING SHOE

Frederick and Bonita's owner was sure that she had left her sandals neatly on the floor. But she frequently found one of these shoes under either a bureau or a bookcase. It surely didn't get there all by itself, right? One day she solved the mystery. She watched Frederick "put on" a shoe. He simply slipped both forepaws under the straps and surfed across the floor with it. And with his typical behavior, during this comical game he landed under either the bureau or the bookcase. That was the end of the line. He climbed out of the shoe and left it where it lay. Maybe Frederick's person should buy him a little skateboard, if the cat has such unusual preferences.

On a sunny winter day I take La Bomba for an outing in the mountains. As snowflakes flutter down from the snowy evergreens, she shakes herself for an instant, but doesn't let that dampen her spirit of adventure. Then with a nimble jump she tries to catch the little snowball I throw for her.

sweet teenagers who have remained with me fill the house with light. Naturally, things are no longer as turbulent as when I had eleven wild little ruffians in the house.

La Bomba, Flori, and Sylvester get along great and have done an outstanding job of fitting into the community. In the meantime the males have been neutered. La Bomba will be my breeding female, and next year she may have her first litter, once she's at least a year old or more—not before.

At the age of eight months, Flori has turned into a powerful cat. He has velvety soft fur and big, amber eyes. He resembles his British Shorthair mother, Isabella, more and more in disposition and appearance: he is gentle, socia-

ble, and a real favorite, especially with children. The only thing we have to watch out for is his gluttony. The only remedy for that is the half-rations diet, which of course he doesn't like.

The top cat Sylvester has inherited the silver undercoat of his mother, Serafina, but with light red tabby striping on top. His bushy tail looks like a squirrel's. He turned out a little small for a Maine Coon mix, for this breed is one of the most imposing ones, but his charm more than makes up for that. He is always in a good mood, and that's contagious to everyone, whether with two or four legs.

La Bomba has remained the star she always was: very intelligent, eager to learn, and enthusi-

Tip

Cats make a distinction between their behavior with other cats and with their humans. In dealing with your indoor tigers, make sure nobody gets shortchanged at playing and stroking.

Christmas is right around the corner, and of course we also have presents for our cats.

astic about everything new. And I can take her with me everywhere, whether on a nature outing, a photo session, or a visit. She seems to like being the center of attention, and is happy when I give her new things to learn. I can walk her almost like a dog, outdoors without a leash. She sometimes runs ahead, hides in a bush, and jumps out like a bolt of lightning when I walk past. But her mother, Serafina, doesn't tolerate it when she forces herself too much into the center of attention. Then there is a little reprimand in the form of a swipe with the paw, which La Bomba respects.

When it's time for petting or playing, I always make sure none of my animals gets short-changed. It's very important to keep anyone from becoming jealous. Cats can live amicably with one another. But the special relationship with their humans is sacred to all cats. No other cat must be allowed to push its way to the front of the line in this regard.

As I type the last lines for this book on my computer, Serafina scratches energetically on my office door. I let her in, and with her tail held high

in a friendly manner she immediately jumps onto the desk. Serafina gnaws on my palm tree, for the rest of the green plants in the house naturally don't taste as good as the one behind a closed door. Then she presses against me and purrs and meows as she rubs her head against me . . .

Okay, Serafina, I get it. It's time for petting, playing, and dinner. Why do people always have to work so much? How can a cat possibly understand? There are much nicer things in life. Yes, as a friend told me a while ago, "If I ever come back in another life, I hope it's as one of your cats."

Advent, advent, there shines a little light, first one, then two . . . It's ice cold outside, and the windows have frosted up. Frederick and Flori play one last time together. Soon each of them will celebrate the coming Christmas holiday with their new families.

The Kitty Before-and-After Quiz

What do these kittens look like when they are adults? Try the following quiz. It's really not so hard. And in the process you will learn to recognize some favorite, exotic cat breeds, including of course the most beloved of all: the domestic shorthair, much more widely known under the term *house cat*.

Here I come on white paws. Who am I?

Who cares about pedigree? Am I not as handsome as any purebred?

This kitten will keep its radiant blue eyes for its entire life.

Right now these two are still small, but later on they will be the biggest.

Blue-gray and soft fur.

In terms of numbers, this little tiger is "breed number one" among cats.

what do these kittens look like...

These kittens come from
an Asian land that gave
this breed its name.

g

This cat's trademarks
are the snub nose and
the long fur later on.

h

i

This kitten inherits its
exotic look from wildcats
in the jungle.

j

Sometimes I have
blue-gray fur, some-
times cream color. Do
you know who I am?

Meow, my fur color is like
that of a wild rabbit, but
I come from Africa.

k

l

Like the little red
cat above, this is
a true long-haired
cat.

...later in Life?

Persian

A long-haired breed with a coat that
requires lots of care; all colorations
are possible. Extreme Persians
have unfortunately been overbred,
especially the typical Peke Face. A calm
disposition and an ideal indoor cat.

Maine Coon

A North American cat with medium-
long hair. Very large, impressive cats
that come in many colors. Tabbies are
the favorites. They like exercise and
are friendly, but have a claim to nobility
in a group of cats. A very popular breed.

House Cat

The familiar domestic shorthair
comes in the widest variety of
fur colors and dispositions.
The most common type is the
tabby cat. A good cat for indoor
living only if it has grown up
inside since kittenhood.

Birman

A breed with medium-long hair, light coat
color, and markings similar to a Siamese.
Markings: pure white paws and blue eyes.
A friendly, sociable cat that is also good
as an indoor cat.

Siamese

Traditional Siamese and Thai (in photo) cats are preferred by many to today's Extreme Siamese. An intelligent, vocal, sensitive, sometimes demanding short-haired breed. Trademarks: blue eyes and the typical Siamese (pointed pattern) markings.

Burmese

This cat came from Burma (now Myanmar) and got its name from the country. An elegant, muscular short-haired cat in chocolate brown, cream, and a few other colors. Disposition: lively, very devoted, and loves to be "number one."

British Shorthair

The British Shorthair comes in all colors, but blue is by far the most numerous and popular. A compact cat with fur like a teddy bear and an easygoing disposition that's well suited to living indoors.

Abyssinian

A muscular short-haired cat whose coat always recalls its ancestors, the dun-colored African wildcat *(Felis silvestris libyca)*. Very alert, devoted, fond of exercise and being the center of attention. They can be trained to perform tricks.

Bengal

This cat resulted from crossing Asian leopard cats and domestic cats. An expensive and exclusive short-haired breed. Disposition: very playful, fond of exercise, but not obtrusive. Gets along well with other cats.

Answers:

1h, 2d, 3c and f, 4a, 5b, 6g, 7e and j, 8k, 9i

Index of Breeds and Subjects

Important Addresses

Cat Associations and Clubs

> American Association of Cat
Enthusiasts (AACE)
P.O. Box 213
Pine Brook, NJ 07058
Phone (973) 335-6717
Web site *www.aaceinc.org*

> American Cat Association (ACA)
8101 Katherine Ave.
Panorama City, CA 91402
Phone (818) 781-5656
Fax (818) 781-5340

> American Cat Fanciers' Association
(ACFA)
P.O. Box 1949
Nixa, MO 65714-1949
Phone (417) 725-1530
Fax (417) 725-1533
Web site *www.acfacat.com*

> Canadian Cat Association (CCA)
289 Rutherford Road, S, #18
Brampton, ON, L6W 3R9
Phone (905) 459-1481
Fax (905) 459-4023
Web site *www.cca-afc.com/*

> Cat Fanciers' Association (CFA)
P.O. Box 1005
Manasquan, NJ 08736
Phone (732) 528-9797
Fax (732) 528-7391
Web site *www.cfainc.org*

> Cat Fanciers' Federation (CFF)
P.O. Box 661
Gratis, OH 45330
Phone (937) 787-9009
Fax (937) 787-4290
Web site *www.cffinc.org*

> The International Cat Association
(TICA)
P.O. Box 2684
Harlingen, TX 78551
Phone (956) 428-8046
Fax (956) 428-8047
Web site *www.tica.org*

> The Traditional Cat Association, Inc.
(TCA)
P.O. Box 178
Heisson, WA 98622-0178
Web site *www.traditionalcats.com*

> United Feline Organization (UFO)
5603 16th Street, W
Bradenton, FL 34207
Phone & Fax (941) 753-8637
Web site *www.unitedfelineorganization.org*

Magazines

Cat Fancy
P.O. Box 6050
Mission Viejo, CA 92690
Phone (800) 365-4421
Web site *www.catfancy.com*

Cats and Kittens
Pet Publishing, Inc.
7-L Dundas Circle
Greensboro, NC 27407
Phone (336) 292-4047
Fax (336) 292-4272
Web site: *www.catsandkittens.com*

Cat Fanciers' Almanac
P.O. Box 1005
Manasquan, NJ 08736-0805
Phone (732) 528-9797

Catnip
Tufts University School of Veterinary
Medicine
P.O. Box 420235
Palm Coast, FL 32142
Phone (800) 829-0926

The Author and Photographer

Monika Wegler

Author Monika Wegler was born on April 21, 1949, in Cologne, Germany. For twenty years she has been working as an independent animal photographer and book author in Munich. She has published more than forty successful animal advisory books and is well known through many calendars and publications in magazines and advertising.

"Animals are dear to my heart, so it's natural for me to support animal and environmental protection projects with part of the proceeds from my work. This time it's the St. Francis of Assisi Animal Shelter in Munich. Here the director, Sylvia Gruber, has set up an exemplary home for stray cats, because unfortunately there are still too many abandoned and sick cats that nobody wants. I would like to thank everyone who gave their all for this book: the editor and proofreader Gabriele Linke-Gruen, the graphic artists Sabine Krohberger and Cordula Schaaf, the producer Susanne Müldorfer, and especially the editor-in-chief Anita Zellner. Thanks also to Dr. Hoffmann in Munich for his veterinary care. Last but not least, I give my heartfelt thanks to my two wonderful mother cats Isabella and Serafina, the male cats Dolittle and Sir Lionel, and to the eleven enchanting kittens, of whom I have kept three, with the result that my cat community has grown to six."